GONE

MYSTERIOUS DISAPPEARANCES

VOLUME 1

GEMMA JADE

Copyright © 2024 by Gemma Jade

All rights reserved.

No part of this book may be reproduced in any form or by any electronic or mechanical means, including information storage and retrieval systems, without written permission from the author, except for the use of brief quotations in a book review.

CONTENTS

Introduction	v
Chapter 1 *Eric Lewis*	1
Chapter 2 *Claudia Kirschhoch*	7
Chapter 3 *Christopher Thompkins*	17
Chapter 4 *James Tedford*	25
Chapter 5 *Ralph W. Heath*	33
Chapter 6 *Owen Parfitt*	45
Chapter 7 *Hannah Upp*	53
Chapter 8 *William Roach*	65
Chapter 9 *Randy Doyle Parscale Jr.*	71
Excerpt	83
Excerpt 2	87
Chapter 10 *Karen Sykes*	95
Chapter 11 *DeOrr Kunz Jr.*	103
Chapter 12 *Daming Xu*	117

Chapter 13   123
Dale Banker

Chapter 14   129
Erin Marie Gilbert

Chapter 15   139
Alfred Beilhartz

Chapter 16   149
Michael David Van Zandt

Chapter 17   155
Philip Kreycik

Chapter 18   161
Kenneth Scott Reed

About the Author   171
Also by Gemma Jade   173

INTRODUCTION

As someone who has dealt with and been enmeshed into the paranormal my entire life, both personally as a medium and professionally as a paranormal non-fiction author and YouTube personality, I've become very accustomed to seeing the supernatural in places where the rest of the world doesn't tend to notice it. That's not to say that every single mystery can be solved by introducing paranormal or otherworldly elements to it, but sometimes that is exactly what's missing in figuring out what really happened. When I first started thinking about writing about mysterious disappearances I understood that it would be a touchy subject for many reasons. I wanted to put my own form of disclaimer here, right in the introduction, for people to understand why I decided to write this book in the way I decided to write it. While the facts are the absolute most important thing I want to convey throughout this book and in each case I cover in it, I also wanted to add something that I think is missing from so many of these cases- and that's a paranormal, supernatural, or otherworldly element. I mean no disrespect to the missing people covered here in this book and I do not mean to diminish the pain and suffering felt by those they left behind. My only goal here is to look beyond the obvious and maybe find some more pieces to the puzzle that have been missing all along. While the facts of each case are presented to the best of my ability to verify them in each case, I am also speculating as to many things that could have happened in each case as well. I am trying to turn some of the unknowns into knowns, and perhaps shed some light on larger issues we have in this world as the veil thins and humanity inches ever closer to what's on the other side of it. Creatures lurking in the woods, otherworldly entities stalking our city streets and anything else that would possibly fit into the missing spaces of these disappearances. With that being said I hope you enjoy this book and start to understand that even in places and at times when we think we are alone or not vulnerable at all is when perhaps we are the most vulnerable and the most crowded we've ever been. Please also keep in mind going forward in this book that the internet is a strange place where anyone can write anything, especially about some of the older cases, and say it's all true. We all have to take everything with a grain of salt and decide for ourselves what we believe the truth to be and so there might be some stories in here that many people believe there isn't enough evidence to back up as even ever having really happened or there may be evidence saying it happened in a completely different way than the evidence I found to say anything to the contrary of that. Just keep an open mind and at the end of the day, whatever you believe, I hope everyone who reads this book gets something from it, even if it's only the stories themselves and how they touch your life.

- Gemma Jade

2024

CHAPTER ONE
ERIC LEWIS

On July 1, 2010, 57 year old Eric Lewis was mountain climbing at Mount Rainier in Washington State. He was accompanied by two men, his climbing companions Don Storm Jr. and Trevor Lane. The climb leader was Don

Storm and the men were heading towards the summit through what's known as Gibraltar Ledges.

Following Don in line on the climbing rope was Trevor Lane in the middle and then Eric Lewis last, at the bottom. Due to very high winds and low visibility the three of them decided that they would move and climb more efficiently if they were to tether themselves together. Once they reached approximately 13,900 feet up the side of the mountain, they decided to regroup, take a break, and talk about what their next moves would be. Don and Trevor, having just glimpsed Eric seconds earlier right below them, pulled themselves over onto the side and waited for him to show up. He never did. They pulled the rope up and instead of finding their climbing companion, they found a butterfly knot and it looked to both of them like he had either unclipped or cut himself free of the rope for unknown reasons. The other two men were surprised but figured there was a rational explanation for why he wasn't there and figuring they'd find him quickly- as there weren't really too many places where he could have gone- they searched for him right away. After all, there had been only mere seconds since the last time they had seen him when they looked down from where they were through the mist and saw him at the bottom of that rope. However, there was no sign of him downhill, near the summit, or anywhere else for that matter so, in not wanting to waste any more time and thinking then that their friend could be in some real danger or trouble, Don and Trevor decided to go back to basecamp and notify the rangers.

An immediate, full scale search was launched as was a search and rescue effort but it was all to no avail. Despite how much snow was on the ground, the only footprints of Erics that were found were the ones from when he had been following his climbing companions up the mountain in the first place, before he had mysteriously gone missing. There were no signs that he had decided to break off from the group and go anywhere on his own, no signs that he had wandered off or that he had turned back. Eric Lewis had simply ceased to exist, or seemingly so, anyway. With all the snow on the ground there should have been at least some additional footprints showing which way Eric had gone and if he had fallen then his body should have immediately been located on the ground below where the other two had last seen him. However, there was none of that and not a single clue was left behind as to where Eric Lewis ended up. Eric's backpack, climbing harness and a snow shovel were found in a snow cave at an altitude of about 13,600 feet. Once again though there were no further clues as to where he ended up or what became of him.

No new information has been uncovered and no

new leads have turned up in regards to this case and to this day Eric Lewis remains a missing person. One of the main questions we ask in the paranormal community is what could have possibly happened to him that the "regular" investigators didn't think of? I discussed this case, not by name but in a generalized way, in my first book *Missing: The Fae Theory* and I did so with the thought that maybe it was the fae who had something to do with this strange and very tragic disappearance. Could these men have been encroaching on fae territory and they decided to retaliate? But why would they only choose Eric when he was there with two other people? Well, I've come to learn through all of my research that the fae are only attracted to certain people and others they couldn't care less about encountering. I couldn't possibly know why this is or what it is that makes some people more desirable targets than others but one thing I think is that it has something to do with possessing something we have no control over but that the fairies want or see as very valuable. There was never a body found in this case and no footsteps leading anywhere. It's not out of the realm of possibility, at least for what we are discussing here, that the fae left his belongings behind when they took him. Maybe he saw them coming and cut his own rope to try and escape them. How else would it be that he didn't make a single sound and seemingly no movements that would alert his friends to the fact that something was wrong? At the very least he could have tugged on the rope to alert them- but there was absolutely nothing. When the fae see something in a human being that they want they will take it without hesitation. Therefore, I personally believe that some fairies spotted Eric and he either tried to cut himself free before they could get to him or they grabbed him and cut him loose themselves and then abducted him. The fae live both in this world and in their own dimension so more than likely he was taken there. For what purpose, I surely have no idea, but that's just one of many theories I have about this particular case. One other thing I thought about was how badly something would have had to have scared him for him to cut himself loose and try to freefall 13,600 feet to the ground, only for him not to make it there. Could this have been the work of extraterrestrials using cloaking technology as I've seen time and time again in many "missing in the woods" type cases? Absolutely. There really is no limit to the possibilities, when using a supernatural lens to view this case, as to what could have happened that day to Eric Lewis.

CHAPTER TWO
CLAUDIA KIRSCHHOCH

It was May of the year 2000 and 29 year old Claudia Kirschoch had what some people would consider a dream job. She was an assistant editor for Frommer's Travel Guides in New York City and Claudia got paid by the company to travel all over the world and write about the exotic places she was visiting and all of the adventures she would go on while there. Sometime in May of 2000 as well, was when Claudia took an all expenses paid trip to Cuba, where she would be staying in the brand new and freshly opened Sandals Resort. First she landed in Montego Bay, Jamaica on May 24th and was getting ready for the first leg of this exclusive vacation. Though Claudia met with some other travel writers while there, they all quickly realized they wouldn't be going to Havana after all because there were some issues with the visas. However, flights back to New York were fully booked for the entire week and so Claudia and a fellow travel writer named Tania Grossinger were stranded in Jamaica. For the time being they were told to "rough it" at the Sandals Beach Resort in Negril until something else could be figured out for them. Negril is known for its tranquility, its gorgeous turquoise blue waters and miles of sandy, white beaches. It was beautiful and Claudia was enjoying herself so much that when Tania got a flight out of there and back to NY, she decided she wanted to spend a few more days there. This would end up being a fateful decision that didn't end well for Claudia and that led to conspiracy theories, a mysterious disappearance and some very bizarre clues left behind.

  Claudia's parents didn't become concerned until June second because they hadn't heard from her in a while and their concern became sheer panic when they called her job and were told that she hadn't ever returned to work and as far as they knew she never came back from Jamaica. Claudia's parents reported her as missing to the authorities and the police immediately launched an investigation. They started where Claudia was last known to have been, at the Sandals Resort in Negril, Jamaica. They were shocked to discover that the last time anyone had seen Claudia Kirschhoch was when she was spotted walking along the beach by a lifeguard. The lifeguard said he saw her on the afternoon of May 27th, walking along the beach in her bathing suit and that she didn't seem upset or under any sort of stress or duress. In fact, she seemed anything but, with the lifeguard describing her as calm and composed and just like she was taking a leisurely, relaxing walk and enjoying her surroundings. However, it's here where Claudia seems to have vanished into thin air. When the authorities spoke to some other staff members at the resort, they were told that Claudia hadn't gone to her room in days and no one had seen her in a while. The search continued and would only get weirder from there. Of course they checked her room at the resort and found that the only things missing from it were the bathing suit that was described as the one she was wearing when she was last spotted on the beach, a portable radio and a t-shirt. Her passport, cell phone, wallet, cash, credit cards, all the rest of her clothes and belongings, including a flight ticket back home to New York, were all in the room untouched. It was as though she planned on going back to her room. Frustratingly, even though the room was considered a potential crime scene, the hotel removed most of Claudia's belongings and even rented it out again to new vacationers. During the time the new tenants were in the room, Claudia's cell phone disappeared mysteriously. Another strange occurrence was that the log book that kept track of all the license plates of the guests and all of the cars entering and exiting the resort, specifically during the time Claudia was there and supposed to be continuing her stay, had managed to go missing somehow. Were these things stolen or were they just misplaced? No one knows still but it is an odd coincidence that book and her phone would go missing right after she did.

The resort claimed not to know how it happened and everyone there pleaded ignorance when questioned about it. Further compounding the whole situation, the investigators found that the CCTV footage from when Claudia was staying at the resort and from the night she disappeared had already been accidentally taped over, leaving investigators with nothing more to go on and with no leads to follow. That is, until they spoke with Tania Grossinger. When police questioned her she told them that during her stay, Claudia had become somewhat close to the bartender at the resort. His name was Anthony Grant and Tania alleged that he and Claudia met on the night before she left to go back to New York to smoke marijuana and to skinny dip together. Of course the authorities had to follow that lead and they looked closely at Anthony Grant, which led to some fairly suspicious findings. Grant had called in sick to work for several days after Claudia disappeared and when he was questioned, he at first tried to claim he didn't know her at all. After being interrogated by the authorities about his relationship with the missing woman, he finally relented and told them that he had met with her on the twenty sixth of May for drinks. The FBI was brought in and they very quickly involved tracker dogs to search Anthony Grant's room. The canines determined that Claudia's scent was all over that room and they also found strands of her hair in his car and a knife with a small amount of something that looked like blood on it. Despite all of this, Grant denied having anything to do with Claudia's disappearance. It was also very bizarre when the FBI almost instantly dropped him as a suspect and didn't even keep him on their radar as a person of interest. The FBI cited a lack of evidence as their reason for not continuing their investigation into Anthony Grant's involvement with the disappearance and also, the fact that he passed more than one polygraph test. Still though, wouldn't you think they would at the very least have the knife tested to see whose blood was on it? Well, they didn't and Anthony Grant was never arrested or charged with any crime in connection to this case. In the eyes of the law Grant was an innocent man but Claudia's parents wholeheartedly disagreed with that determination. They insisted that he must have known something and they also accused the resort of concealing information to protect its integrity with other tourists. However, their accusations and pleas fell on deaf ears and the FBI and other authorities quickly moved on.

    The FBI and investigators weren't the only ones who weren't listening to Claudia's distraught parents. They approached the resort themselves but received no cooperation. Because of that, Claudia's parents felt they had no choice but to launch a lawsuit against the resort for allowing the contamination of evidence of a crime scene, which they claimed the resort had done when they rented out Claudia's room before the investigation was finished, causing her cell phone to be stolen. The lawsuit asserted that the resort contaminated evidence, mishandled items that had gone missing, a lack of proper security measures, and for allegedly withholding pertinent information regarding their daughter's disappearance. Of course, with all of this going on, the media was having a field day. The resort was portraying Claudia to the media as a reckless and wild party girl who smoked marijuana and claimed she was an irresponsible foreigner who drank too much and got high. They basically accused Claudia of inviting trouble to her. The Jamaican authorities were involved at this point as well but they had drawn their own conclusions, seemingly out of the clear blue sky and at random, with no actual, tangible evidence to back up their claims. They asserted that Claudia had either drowned or voluntarily run away to start a new life I reiterate- there was absolutely no evidence for either one of those theories, but still, they stuck to their story. In fact, all of the water anywhere near where Claudia was last seen was shallow and had no strong currents. Also, there was nothing at all going on in or about her life that would warrant anyone thinking she was so desperate to leave it all behind that she would engage in this gigantic plot to disappear and leave her loved ones grieving her. Further confusing things were the several sightings of Claudia after she was reported as missing in the more remote areas of the region, with some alleged witnesses claiming they had seen her and she had been accompanied by a Rastafarian man, seemingly happy and relaxed in his presence. Unfortunately, none of those reported sightings have ever been able to be officially confirmed and Claudia Kirschhoch hasn't been seen since that day in May when the lifeguard reportedly saw her walking calmly on the beach. She was declared legally dead in the year 2002.

Throughout the investigation Jamaican officials were allegedly very uncooperative and they refused to allow the family access to any of their files on Claudia's disappearance and they also didn't divulge much, if any, pertinent information about the disappearance or their investigation into it. No one knows how they came to their official conclusions except today that most people think they just wanted to get the case closed and the media off their backs so that it didn't affect the revenue from tourism in that area. That's all alleged though and like I said, no one really knows what their investigation entailed. Due to their alleged silence, Claudia's mother said, "Nobody's saying that Claudia was murdered. She died. How that happened is a matter of speculation. Without cooperation from the Jamaican authorities, it's very, very hard to get the truth." The investigation into Claudia's disappearance has since been closed, no new leads or clues were ever discovered, no suspects were ever found or named and the resort never had to answer for their negligence or for any of it and continued with business as usual. There are nothing but questions left behind, confounded by a whole bunch of rumors and rampant speculation. There are many people who believe Anthony Grant should have been looked at more closely or at the very least his knife should have been tested to see whose blood was on it. What happened to her phone? Did it contain any clues? What are the odds that all of the CCTV footage only from Claudia's stay would "accidentally" be recorded over at the same time the log with all the license plates of the vehicles coming and going went missing, somehow? Astronomical, I know, but still and all Claudia's family have been given no answers. As I said in the beginning I have no intention of adding to anyone's pain and suffering but I do have my own opinions about this case and I'd like to share those with you now. I am looking at this case, just like all the others with a supernatural and paranormal- an otherworldly lens.

There are many cases, as you'll see with the further along you get in this book, where someone goes missing without a trace near water. It was almost an epidemic with young college age students leaving bars at one point in time and we are going to discuss that too at some point, some of those cases, but what about the water? There are many of us in this community that believe there are things going on under the ocean, the seas of our world and many other water sources across the globe, that human beings have no idea about or at the very least no proof of. Is there some form of extraterrestrial or cryptozoological life that's underneath these waters? That are based there that are snatching human beings and bringing them down into the depths with them, for whatever reason? While this case doesn't seem as much like it could be paranormal like so many of the others, I included it here mainly to show how easily, quickly and completely a whole person can disappear into thin air while only a second before they had been quietly and calmly relaxing on the beach. The beauty of the water and the sandy shores that attract so many of us to it, could possibly be what attracts these otherworldly things to it as well and there's no telling what their intentions are because as of right now, human beings have only begun to explore a speck of the oceans and waters of our world, in the grand scheme of things. I hope one day the truth is told about what happened to this poor young lady and at the very least I hope her family finds the peace and closure they desperately need and very much deserve.

CHAPTER THREE

CHRISTOPHER THOMPKINS

On January 25th, 2002, 20 year old Christopher Thompkins was just going about his normal day and living his life working as a surveyor while living with his mom. He woke up and after saying goodbye to his mother, he left for his job at 8:10. He met up with the three other members of the four man surveyor team and set about their daily survey work in a slightly wooded area off of County Line Road, near Highway 85, in Ellerslie, Georgia, in the United States. The team worked and moved as a unit, with each man spaced about fifty feet apart and working their way through the forest in the same direction as one another. Christopher was the last man in the unit's line but he was within eyesight of the man in front of him and was in constant audible communication with all of the men throughout the day. At some point in time, the surveyor who was in front of him glanced back towards where Christopher should've been standing, as they had just been talking to one another only a minute or so before that, but he saw, strangely, that Christopher not only wasn't in line anymore, but that he was nowhere in sight in the area surrounding them either. He immediately called to the others and the three of them searched the area high and low for their co-worker but they couldn't find him anywhere and he wasn't responding to them calling his name either. One of Christopher's work boots was hanging from a barbed wire fence that was nearby where they had been standing. The barbed wire fence stretched throughout the area but there was no sign of his other boot anywhere. This was all very confusing as it was no more than a minute since the man in front of him had been speaking to him, turned his head and then turned back again when he noticed Christopher had vanished. Lying on a patch of grass near the fence were his work tools, twelve cents and some blue fiber thought to have been from his work pants. There were no other clues and it seemed to the men as though their friend and co-worker had merely blinked out of existence while they were all standing nearby, without having seen or heard anything at all.

However, things would only get stranger from there because it wasn't until around one in the afternoon that the other three men would finally report Christopher as missing. That was nearly four hours after they had initially discovered he was gone. The men didn't call the authorities right away, and in fact their first call was to their boss, who they told Christopher had "vanished." His mother wasn't notified of the disappearance until nearly 4:15 that night too. Once his mother was informed, she was told by the authorities that she had to wait twenty four hours before they would officially open any type of investigation into what happened to him and eventually, once that time had passed, there was a more extensive and intense investigation launched, but nothing more was ever found. It wasn't until months later that Christopher's other work boot would be found. A man who lived nine hundred yards from where Thompkins had gone missing had only by chance found the boot there on his private property. The question remains, how did this young man just go missing, seemingly vanishing into thin air, in the blink of an eye and in full view of the other men? How had he gotten away so fast and why were there never any signs or sightings of him anywhere?

One of the main theories that's sprung up over the years was that there had to have been some sort of foul play involved here, regarding the other men he had been working with that day. People wondered why it took the men so long to call their boss and report that Christopher had vanished and speculated that it was possible they had killed him or otherwise done something terrible to him, and that four hours was more than enough time to have hidden his body and other belongings. However, none of them were ever found to have any notice for wanting to hurt Thompkins, there were no signs of foul play anywhere in the area and none of those men were ever seriously considered by the authorities to have been connected to the disappearance in any way. None of the other surveyors were ever seriously interrogated or investigated about any of it. Many people also thought that it was possible Christopher merely walked off the job because he wanted to go missing and that he was out there somewhere, living a whole new life. Christopher's boss alleged that he had been acting strangely, different than usual, in the days leading up to his disappearance and those claims seemed to back up that particular theory. However, Christopher's mother, who lived with him, adamantly denied that her son had been behaving out of his normal character and said everything was perfectly normal until the moment he disappeared. She told the Ledger-Enquirer, "Chris lived with me and I saw him every day. There was neither strange behavior on his part, nor any distress." Honestly, I'm inclined to listen to his mother here as I think she would have noticed if there had been anything strange going on with her son because they did live together and seemed to have a very close relationship. Other family members who knew him well and all of his friends said that he was a happy, well-adjusted person, and his co-workers seconded those emotions by saying that he was hard working, respectable and dependable. If he walked away, then how would he have possibly done that within full view of the other men? At the very least the man closest to him, with whom he had just been talking to less than sixty seconds before he vanished, would have been able to see him walking off and possibly climbing that fence etc. Also, why would he leave one boot behind? Why were any of the seemingly bizarre clues left behind, if he had done all of this as part of a carefully crafted plot to start a new life somewhere and put his mother and other loved ones through hell? It doesn't make any sense.

Some people have suggested that perhaps Christopher had been the victim of some sort of animal predation but in my opinion at least, and most people who know more about such things than I do tend to agree, there would have been more signs of a struggle, he would have been seen being attacked and at the very least the man closest to him would have heard him screaming. There would have been blood, kicked up dirt or grass. There was no evidence to support any of the theories I've mentioned so far and honestly, there was no evidence to support anything having happened to him other than something unseen possibly grabbing him and getting him over that fence and out of there so quickly that it only took the mere blink of an eye for it to all be started, done and over with. That's why I included it here in this book. Like with all of the other cases in this book I am not going to say one way or another the exact thing that I believe happened here but I will speculate about various supernatural forces that could be to blame. Specifically in this case I would like to bring all of your attention to the fact that, more and more in recent years, we in the paranormal community have been seeing more and more encounters with cloaked or translucent humanoid beings that we know are there but that we can't see unless looking at them in the direct sunlight. Yes, it would have looked like quite a sight to the other men in the crew to see Christopher just be picked up and carried over the fence, possibly hooking his leg on it and thereby tearing the fabric of his pants in the meantime and losing a boot but hear me out.

We also know in this community that there are also entities that are able to really do a number by playing strange tricks on our perceptions and especially on our perception of time. What if time stood still for just a moment and that's when the creature or entity, whatever it was, swooped in and grabbed the poor and unassuming young man from his spot there in the survey line? No one would have been the wiser once time started up again and we all know that this type of phenomenon only usually affects one person in a group and everyone else is none the wiser about it. That's one of the main reasons most people don't talk about these types of events in the first place and the few brave souls who do experience something like this, who live to tell about it and then do go on to talk about what happened to them, are normally cast off as crazy people who are going through some sort of crisis or mental break or something. I don't know what happened here, but in looking at this case through the lens of the paranormal, I would say that something saw Christopher and decided to take him and doing that in front of three other men was something that could easily be gotten around. I think the most likely scenario is the one I mentioned before where whatever it was stopped our clocks for just a moment, and took him, probably kicking and screaming, to wherever it was that it needed or wanted him to go. I don't believe most people taken this way are killed, but please keep in mind this is just my own speculation and paranormal hypothesis. I hope and pray that some answers come for the family and at the very least they find some reason for this that they can live with, until one day maybe they can grasp the full truth of what happened to their loved one.

CHAPTER FOUR

JAMES TEDFORD

68-Year-Old Veteran Missing After Boarding Bus in St. Albans City

BENNINGTON, Dec. 7—State Police here have just discovered that James Tedford, 68, a veteran at the Soldiers' Home here, failed to return as scheduled last Thursday.

Gen. Reginald Buzzell reported to the State Police today that Tedford had been visiting his wife in Franklin. Relatives accompanied him to a bus in St. Albans, and that was the last that has been seen of him.

A State Police broadcast gives Tedford's description as wearing a cap, grey suit and army overcoat. He is five feet, five inches tall and weighs about 116 pounds.

In the 1940's a fifty six year old man named James Tedford (sometimes spelled Tetford) was living a quiet and peaceful life in a small town in Franklin, Vermont named Fletcher Town. James was a war veteran and his wife's name was Pearl. Pearl was much younger than James at just 28 years old. Pearl and James were said to be a sweet couple, even somewhat unassuming and they lived an uneventful and "normal" life. That is until World War Two came along and James decided to go off for a second tour. We should note here that when James left for his tour in the military, he and Pearl were getting along great and by all accounts they were both looking forward to the day when he would return home and they could continue with life as they knew it and move on. This is exactly what happened too when James returned from war. He and Pearl seemed more in love than ever before and were happy to have been reunited and that James had returned in one piece. There were no signs at all that would account for what happened next. It seems James Tedford isn't the only one in this story to have disappeared seemingly without a trace. Shortly after returning home from his tour of duty, James walked into his house to find an odd scene. Pearl was nowhere to be found and she should have been there, as she always was. She hadn't mentioned she would be going anywhere and she always let James know where she was going and when she would be back. It seems however that perhaps Pearl herself wasn't aware she would be going anywhere either as there was a half prepared dinner out on the kitchen counters. It's reasonable to assume that Pearl had been in the process of putting it all together and cooking it for the two of them when something interrupted her. Because everything else was in order and despite this being very unlike his wife, James didn't panic at first and just assumed that she had stepped out, perhaps having forgotten an ingredient for the dinner she was preparing or something of that nature. He waited for her to return but she never did. By the time nightfall rolled around and Pearl still hadn't returned, James decided to go and speak to some of his neighbors to see if any of them had seen her that day.

More than a few friends and neighbors told James they had seen Pearl at the local Amoco station earlier in the afternoon and that she seemed perfectly normal. She was her polite and friendly self to all who encountered her. She was even said to have been in good spirits and not in the least under any duress at all. The next day, when she still hadn't returned and he hadn't heard from her, James finally notified the local police. The authorities immediately went to the Tedford home to investigate and question James but they could find no trace of Pearl anywhere in the home, on the property or in any of the surrounding areas. It was as though she were standing at the kitchen counter preparing a meal for her and her husband and POOF! Vanished into thin air.

The authorities almost immediately started to speculate that perhaps Pearl had run off on James but that didn't make much sense as she hadn't left a note and furthermore- why in the world would she leave behind the half prepared meal? Also, her demeanor that day as described by people who knew her, some who knew her well, didn't lend credence to her having just got up and run off on her husband and her life. Pearl was never seen or heard from again and this threw James into a deep depression. He was almost despondent and missed his wife and mourned for her tirelessly. He could never understand what could have possibly happened to her to have made her leave the way she did and with no evidence left behind. He would sit and stare at the wall, almost non blinking for hours on end and went days without moving out of his chair. Eventually it all became too much for James and he couldn't stand to be in the house he had once shared with his beloved and missing wife anymore. In 1947 he moved to the Soldier's Retirement Home in Bennington, Vermont. It's said that while there he made no attempt to make friends and basically kept to himself all the time. He did have a few relatives left but they lived about 8 hours away by bus in St. Albans, Vermont. The trip was long and went through a pretty rugged wilderness area throughout Route 7 at the time. James did go and visit them every once in a while for a change of scenery but he was never able to recover from Pearl's vanishing and it was like he was a whole different person altogether. How terrible to make it through two such incredibly dangerous, terrifying, and harsh tours of war, especially in those days, only to be personally ruined because of an ominous and tragic mystery that there's no hope of ever solving involving someone you love dearly? In December of 1949, some of those relatives invited James to come and visit for a few days and he agreed.

James took the long trip and made it to his destination unharmed and, physically at least, in good health. It was the journey home that would become another one of the mysteries of the so-called Bennington Triangle. It should be said that James Tedford, at least since losing his beloved wife Pearl, was a sour and tempestuous, quiet man and the passengers who rode the bus with him that day, as he made his way back to the retirement home, said that was exactly how he seemed. Nothing was amiss as far as what the authorities could gather when they started investigating how James Tedford, an old veteran on a bus packed with people could literally evaporate into thin air. But let's back up just a moment. James never returned to the retirement home and his absence was immediately noticeable. The staff and some other residents knew when he was expected to be back and grew immediately concerned when he didn't show up because he was nothing if not punctual. There were fifteen other passengers on the bus that day and the bus driver confirmed he had gotten on the bus. The driver had even shown the investigators where James had been sitting during the long trip back. All of the cash he had on him at the time, his luggage and all of the rest of his belongings were left stowed away on the bus. The only thing that was missing was James himself. His belongings being left behind was more confirmation that he had in fact boarded the bus and took a seat. According to multiple witnesses, James was last seen sleeping in his seat on the bus and hadn't gotten off at any of the stops along the way. The bus driver attested to this and said he always took notice of the passengers who got off the bus at the stops, especially when there were only fifteen of them on a bus that held many more seats. However, it's also said that aside from his boarding, taking his seat and then being seen sleeping soundly, James was pretty nondescript and there was no other reason for anyone to notice him or pay attention to what he was doing. Even still, if he didn't get off of the bus at any of the stops, how and when did he get off then? He certainly wasn't able to get out or off of a moving bus without being noticed. It was also snowing very heavily at the time of the trip and disappearance.

James Tedford is another person who seems to have been here one minute and gone the next. How does a whole person, a grown man who was tough and gruff and made weary by life and war, who kept to himself and greatly missed his beloved wife- who also went missing mysteriously and seemed to just vanish- disappear into thin air while on a crowded bus in front of 16 witnesses? It should also be mentioned this disappearance took place in what is known today as the Bennington Triangle. The Bennington Triangle claimed a known total of five people between the five short years of 1945 and 1950 and the disappearances and strange happenings continue to this day. The Bennington Triangle itself is usually the most common explanation for what happened to James but that's just it- there's no explanation for why all of these strange vanishings and other happenings happen there either. I don't want to break down the Bennington Triangle mystery in this book, but I do want to at least take the area into consideration as we move forward into what I think could have happened to James. A lot of the cases I've written about so far have to do with otherworldly entities and extraterrestrials, but what about other realms and dimensions too? We still don't know for sure that aliens come from other planets and many people, me included, believe that even if they did the other planets and galaxies are merely other realms accessible to most of them but not to humans yet. I believe Pearl's random and bizarre disappearance had a lot to do with why James was more than likely chosen to be taken the way he was. I speculate that perhaps there's certain places in the world where these otherworldly beings are more able to stop time and/or turn it forward and backwards at will. I would love a happy ending to this tragedy and it makes sense to me that maybe Pearl had been taken by some race of interdimensional travelers, for whatever reason chose her but maybe she was just a despondent for not being able to live and grow old with her one true love that they, being mostly compassionate beings, decided finally to take James along as well and reunite them. I believe a lot of people who go missing in the woods were chosen for something about them that we don't understand yet to be taken to a place equally as mystifying to us but that's just like our Earth. Maybe some otherworldly and supernatural force took these two love birds and brought them to a timeline where they were able to finally be together and their bodies or any traces of them were never found because they were able to be happy enough with that to assimilate to this new place as long as they would be together. Maybe, James and Pearl were brought together by their unique and enduring love and finally got to have their happily ever-after.

CHAPTER FIVE

RALPH W. HEATH

Ralph W. Heath was a park ranger at Baxter State Park in Maine, United States who allegedly died of hypothermia himself while attempting to rescue a woman who was lost on Mount Katahdin in 1963. On

Monday, October 28th of that same year, two women, Helen Mower, and Margaret Ivusic, both from Concord, Massachusetts, took the Cathedral Trail and climbed Baxter Peak on the mountain. They reached the summit and stopped to have lunch at around 1:30 in the afternoon. When the two friends decided to start their hike again and head back down, they had a small argument over the route Margaret wanted to take. Helen simply wanted to go back the way they came but Margaret wanted to "bushwhack", which very simply put, means to leave the established trail or "get off the beaten path". Helen knew how risky this was, although Margaret had more hiking experience than she did, it wasn't by much and only three years total. She thought it way too dangerous and stormed off to take Dudley trail which was the original trail they had taken to get there. She decided to let her friend make her own mistakes and go her own way. It was a decision she would live to regret.

Margaret on the other hand thought she was taking a shortcut and laughed off her friend's warnings. They went their separate ways and agreed to meet at the Chimney Pond lean-to. When Helen reached the final destination and saw there was no sign of Margaret she decided to wait, figuring it would have taken her longer to get there in the first place, but got very worried very quickly. Though it was a nice and sunny day out that day, a nor'easter was blowing in and the weather was about to take a turn very quickly for the worse. She started calling for Margaret and was pleasantly surprised when she heard her friend respond and start calling back, despite the fact she was asking for help, because at least she knew her friend was nearby and she could go and get whatever help she needed. Margaret yelled that she was not hurt but was stuck in the treacherous terrain and it was impossible for her to be able to continue on or turn back. She pleaded with Helen to go and get some help for her. Helen, of course, agreed to do that.

This is when Helen made her way to the ranger's station and encountered ranger Ralph Heath having dinner. She explained the situation and Ralph immediately knew how dangerous that particular path was and how serious a problem they had. He was however, thanking his lucky stars, in his mind at least, that there hadn't been any snowfall yet, as any other year for as far back as he could remember there would have been snow covering the mountain for weeks at that point in the year. Ralph followed Helen back to Chimney Point and yelled out in the direction of Margaret and instructed her, in a very calm and clear voice, to stay where she was and not try to move or go anywhere. He assured her that help was on the way. With the wind increasing like it was, Ralph knew that the situation could go from scary to deadly in a matter of just seconds. He had to act fast. He took Helen back to the ranger's station and radioed his supervisor, Helen Taylor, and told him there was a hiker stranded in the upper basin on the mountain.

A little background on Mr. Ralph Heath, to show what a brave man he was and how he was definitely not someone to shy away from trouble. He served in World War Two and was honorably discharged. However, a house fire destroyed everything he owned but the clothes on his back, including his discharge papers. He was redrafted to serve in the Korean war before anyone could verify he had already been discharged and had finished his service. Ralph went without hesitation to serve his country only for his wife to decide she didn't want to deal with another tour, especially one he shouldn't have had to have gone on in the first place, and she filed for divorce. This was a man who was seeking solitude and peace in his life after all of this tragedy and heartbreak and who absolutely loved his job as a ranger and the beauty of the mountain.

Despite the weather outside becoming more and more perilous and the orders from the supervising ranger that they had to wait until morning to attempt any kind of search and rescue, Ralph decided the risk to Margaret was too great, leaving her out there all alone at night. Snow was definitely coming and a lot of it. He decided to attempt the rescue himself, despite it being nightfall and dark outside. The temperature had drastically dropped as well. He borrowed Helen's backpack and filled it with essentials such as food, a sleeping bag, water, a parka, and extra clothes. He also took eighty feet of rope and at eleven pm that same night, headed alone down Dudley Trail. It wasn't until five hours later, at around four in the morning that he reported back to Helen. He told her he had spoken to Margaret about an hour after heading out and was able to obtain her location, and that he had again told her to stay put and assured her help was on the way. She reiterated she was uninjured but very cold. More than a little scared as well I'm sure. He told Helen that Margaret was near the waterfall and he wouldn't be able to reach her without more rope and more people. This was an area that even ice climbers considered treacherous and dangerous. Ralph was also extremely concerned because Margaret was refusing to stay and wait for help to arrive and was determined to find a way out herself, for fear she would freeze to death before anyone would be able to rescue her. After reassuring Helen and telling her what was going on, he contacted his supervisor, Heron Taylor and made him aware as well. Taylor dispatched the Maine Forest Service, two additional park rangers and a Maine game warden.

By six that morning, Tuesday the 29th, an icy rain began to fall and the wind had picked up drastically. Ralph Heath ate his breakfast and then informed Helen Mower of his plans. He was going to ascend the ravine from Chimney Pond, climb straight up the headwall and into the waterfall where he would provide comfort to Barbara and, if he couldn't manage to rescue her himself, at least she wouldn't be scared and alone, and he would wait with her until the additional resources arrived to get them both out. He refused to leave her alone out there. He was clearly putting himself at great risk, knowing it was unlikely he would be able to do anything but just sit with Margaret and wait, yet he did it anyway. He was truly a hero. While the plan was very reasonable, and despite being a chain smoker, Ralph was in great shape and a capable hiker and climber, it would still be a significant risk to take regardless of whether he waited or attempted to rescue her himself. However, he had hiked Dudley Trail four times in the last twenty four hours and it was a very strenuous and hard trail to get through. He was absolutely exhausted and shouldn't have been doing any more hiking or climbing without getting some much needed rest. This would after all be a trail less climb he was attempting to make! He wasn't going to leave Margaret alone so the admonishments and earnings from his co-workers and even Helen fell on deaf ears.

Ralph reached Margaret just as Hurricane Ginny reached the mountain. He sat with her for a little while and the two hunkered down. A Ranger Sargent set out on foot towards Chimney Pond as well and stated that, by the time he got to just the basin, the conditions were white out with gale force winds. By noon, not even the Jeeps could make it to the trailhead, there was eighteen inches of snow on the ground already and more falling fast. He even reported that, only halfway up the mountain, his clothes had frozen solid and literally cracked at the elbows. Having no visibility and facing merciless winds, not to mention the condition of his clothing, he was forced back down the mountain. He stated he knew that both Ralph and Margaret were in some very serious trouble as help could no longer get to them. It would be impossible for them to help themselves as well.

The following morning, Wednesday October 30, 1963, Warden Supervisor David Priest returned to Roaring Brook and set up what we today call an incident command center and had at least thirty five people there working at all times. All different avenues of help were brought in and explored but nobody could do anything as the snow was still accumulating, and fast, on Friday morning. It was November first now and five full days since Margaret had gotten herself stuck and four whole days since Ralph Heath had joined her to provide comfort and possible rescue, and we know now in hindsight that he was unable to do the latter. On Saturday, November second, all teams, and persons involved decided that any rescue attempts were futile and they were simply wasting resources at that point. They thought it very likely they would be on a body recovery mission.

A Mr. William Lowell Putnam the third was one of the most experienced mountaineers in the country at the time and had been helping with the rescue efforts since Friday. Finally on Sunday November third he made the statement that he believed Ralph and Margaret had most likely died on Tuesday and reiterated the waste of resources should they continue on this impossible trek to try and save them. It wasn't until almost six months later in April of 1964 that Margaret Ivusic's body was found and finally able to be brought down the mountain and sent home. Even at this time though they needed chemical salts to melt the ice so as not to damage the corpse in any way and the rescue still took an additional three days. It was found during autopsy that Margaret was severely injured and hadn't survived more than a few hours due to the extreme blood loss. Her official cause of death was exsanguination. Two weeks later on May fifteenth they finally found Ralph's body. He was found four hundred feet above where Margaret was found. They airlifted him out of there. His autopsy showed nothing at all to point to his cause of death. The coroner stated, "It looks as if he simply sat down and went to sleep."

Now I know that this is a case where the people didn't necessarily disappear but I would like to point out a few things about it that somewhat back up my statements that something supernatural is at play in a lot of these areas in general, and when it comes to people vanishing within them. I think it's important we go over a few of the facts here. First, if Margaret had died very quickly- within a few hours- after getting stuck where she was, how was she yelling to Ralph hours later? She had severed an artery in her leg and would have bled out within just minutes. She was still calling out and answering him hours after she initially got stuck. How is this even possible? She had called out to Helen as well even before that and we know neither one was under any kind of duress or sick at all so they couldn't have been hallucinating. There were no other bodies found in the area that time and no one else had come forward claiming to have been stuck up there and answering either Helen or Ranger Heath who could have been mistaken for Margaret either. This is very strange but becoming more and more common. Either search and rescue workers will hear the calls of people who are missing only to never be able to find the location of where the calls are coming from or, the person who is stuck or lost will hear search and rescue and never seem to be able to find them either. The weather coming on so suddenly and so strong all at once is another very familiar factor when talking about the missing and the woods and or mountains. In fact, they were weeks late for any snow at all and the weather started out that day as sunny and warm. This is just one of the many parameters many people are now looking at while investigating the strange deaths and disappearances in the woods. Obviously that includes me. How and why did it all come on so very suddenly, almost remarkably so? I guess we'll never really know, but just sitting around and pretending like this all makes any sort of sense is just as ludicrous in my opinion.

Let's just pretend for a moment that there was something supernatural or otherworldly happening or at play here. I believe that something lured Ranger Heath up to that place once it saw something in him that it wanted or possibly that it needed. I know those are very general and broad statements but that's the nature of my business. That's the nature of the paranormal. I wonder if perhaps it saw something in his energy field or perhaps in his soul- he was another exceptional person who had been through great heartache, who had done two tours in different wars, and he was a hero who never broke down and was still willing to put his life on the line for strangers. To me, that's more than exceptional and the more I look into these cases, the more I see people like this being taken, disappearing, or dying under mysterious circumstances. Also, what was his cause of death? How is it even acceptable for a coroner to say they have no idea what actually caused the death and, or so it seems to me, for them to just take a guess that he possibly could have died of hypothermia- maybe? I don't understand how this counts as any sort of reasonable answer in real life, but then again, it isn't really the reality we all know that we are dealing with in most of these cases, is it?

CHAPTER SIX

OWEN PARFITT

Location where Owen Parfitt disappeared.

When Owen Parfitt would tell stories of his life, as he sat in his wheelchair on his front porch in his old age, he would tell of so many wild adventures. He claimed to have bedded more women than he could count, participated in battles against pirates and so many other tales that seemed to be, possibly, a bit "tall." He knew the people who would sit and visit with him thought perhaps he was embellishing his youth a bit, but that never stopped Owen from weaving a great yarn for anyone who would listen. In the 1760's Owen was crippled and said he owed that mostly to the glory days of his youth. His favorite pastime was sitting out on his porch in his chair, talking to anyone who would stop to listen to and converse with him and just being out in the fresh air and sun. Owen Parfitt lived with his elderly sister who was just a few years older than him but who was able and willing to take him in and care for him as he could no longer do a lot of things for and by himself. They lived in a small cottage in a little village called Susannah in Shepton Mallet in southwest England. While there isn't much information as to what happened to the now sixty year old man that turned him into a virtual cripple, it's said it weighed heavily on him as he was once a vibrant and active man, not to mention extremely independent. However, what eventually happened to Owen- how the story of his life ends- could very well be called his final adventure and it definitely had everyone talking about him, which is what he always strived for. He wanted to be memorable, even if in some small way and even if it meant lying about all of the crazy and wild things he had seen and done in his long lifetime. Whether done on purpose or completely by some bizarre twist of fate, we are obviously still talking about Owen Parfitt to this day, centuries later in fact. This is a tale Owen himself would have loved to tell. Because of how long ago this all took place the dates are also hard to pin down. Some say it happened in July of 1763 and others say it all went down during the summer of 1768. Regardless of the date, one thing is certain, Owen Parfitt was there one moment and gone the very next as if blinking an eye could cause someone to vanish into the air surrounding them.

One warm summer evening in the summertime of either 1763 or 1768, Owen wanted to go outside and sit on his front porch. It was midafternoon and a beautiful day by all accounts. It was one of those days where people may actually wonder if anything bad could possibly happen- but on this day something definitely did. Owen wanted to get out of his wheelchair and sit on one of the chairs his sister had on the front porch for days just like this. Because of his own inability to get himself out of his chair and into the one on the porch, Owen's sister called on a neighbor to help her get him outside. He needed to be lifted and carried out onto the porch and his elderly sister certainly couldn't achieve this all on her own but she was more than willing to oblige her brother. She and the neighbor got Owen comfortably outside and into one of the chairs so he could catch some sun and breathe the fresh air. The neighbor conversed for a bit with Owen and then went on his way and when Owen's sister turned to go inside, her brother was sitting comfortably and placidly in the porch chair. That was the last time she would ever see her brother. Across the road, within earshot of him, Owen could see some men working on a farm and they could certainly see and hear him. Basically, if anyone approached Owen and tried doing him harm or abducting him, not only would his sister just inside the front door have heard him but it's certain that these laborers also would have not only seen but heard it all happen right away. But nobody saw or heard a thing when Owen suddenly disappeared. A storm was rolling in and Owen's sister went back outside just a short time later, merely a few minutes from when she first left him out there, to try and get him back inside. It was said to be coming in quite quickly, this storm, and she was obviously concerned with her brother being caught out there on the chair, not able to move the bottom half of his body of his own accord. However, once she was outside and on the front porch where her brother sat just a very short while ago, she noticed he was gone. Owen was nowhere in sight. His unnamed sister asked the farmhands if they had seen or heard anything but they all said they hadn't and they all went about searching for him on the property. However improbable it was that Owen would have been anywhere other than that chair on the front porch due to his conditions, it was a much more reasonable thought than that he had up and somehow vanished into thin air.

His sister got the farmhands and several neighbors to help her search the rest of the property and beyond but it was all to no avail. Owen was nowhere to be found and there was no rhyme or reason as to where he could have gone. There was no trace of him either and this case still remains unsolved to this very day. What in the world could have happened to Owen Parfitt on that warm sunny day so long ago? There are some theories floating around, of course, but keep in mind they are just that- theories and there is no evidence to back any of them up. There was also no evidence of foul play. This is the exact type of disappearance I set out to talk about here in this book. Where do I even begin? The property was somewhat wooded and had some forested areas surrounding it but again the details are a bit hazy and somewhat all over the place. Someone or something had to go and take this man off of that porch chair and carry him, one way or another, to some other place. However, no one saw or heard anything and there were no traces of him or any evidence as to what could have possibly happened to him left behind. When I hear stories about people disappearing in this way and trust me it happens a lot more often than most people think it does, I always imagine the person being taken upwards. With everything we know in this community about how UFOs and those in charge of those types of craft operate, we know they normally have no qualms about plucking an innocent and defenseless, unsuspecting human being right out of the here and now and taking them wherever they need or want them to go. Some people say bigfoot could have gotten him or even some other wild animal but it couldn't have possibly been anything that ordinary because there would have been evidence left behind. It couldn't have been human beings because where would they have been hiding and how would they have made it so no one saw or heard them abducting this old man? No ransom calls ever came in to Owen's sister and in fact no evidence ever turned up one way or another explaining where Owen had disappeared to. In my professional opinion based on all the research I've done into so many different beings and entities in this community throughout the years, is that Owen was more than likely another person who was abducted by

UFOs and them either intended all along to keep him or something went horribly wrong.

I see time and again that there are people who say they were taken by extraterrestrials by way of being beamed up or otherwise into a UFO and then the creatures and beings inside heal them and send them on their way. What if that's what happened here? What if Owen either shared some DNA with some otherworldly beings and they wanted to help him live out the rest of his life without suffering and while being able to get around like he used to, which was one of his main wishes for himself? I've also seen many reports from people who say that they had been abducted for healing purposes, as that's what they were told, but the entities involved told them that despite their best efforts, there was nothing that they could do to save them after all. I've even seen a handful of cases where the healings went horribly wrong and the person only ended up traumatized from the efforts. Owen's case is different because I don't see any reason why they would have wanted to hurt or harm him and to me it just feels more like they would have wanted to help him out. Believe it or not, that's the case eight times out of ten. We mainly hear horror stories that, at the heart of them, aren't really so horrific but the experience itself is what makes the whole thing traumatic. The healings can be painful and terrifying but most people never regret their experience, for better or for worse, because of the energy and just the overall demeanor of the beings claiming to want to help them. I wonder if this is a case where Owen, with his interesting and adventurous personality, was abducted for healing purposes and decided he would have a better time staying with the creatures there to cure or heal him than sitting paralyzed and dependent on his sister for whatever time he had left here on this planet. Whatever you believe, at the end of the day, there's no way he just got up and walked away. Another thing I found so fascinating about this case is how no one heard or saw anything at all and he really was there one moment and gone the next. One other reason I'm convinced it was extraterrestrial or at the very least otherworldly in nature is because of that fact. I've seen case after case where time stopped completely for everyone around the person who was the subject of the abduction and only once the person was gone did time start again for the others, mainly with them being none the wiser. Time works differently in other realms and dimensions and in outer space too, if that's where you believe ETs and UFOs are from, and perhaps Owen did show back up one day, only he did so in an alternate dimension or on a different timeline, far in the future, where no one would have immediately recognized who he was.

CHAPTER SEVEN
HANNAH UPP

Back in 2008 Hannah Upp was a seemingly normal schoolteacher who, at first glance, seemed like she was living a regular "normal" life. She taught at the Thurgood Marshall Academy, which is a public school in Harlem, NY, and she had no history of behavioral problems, problems in or within her family and she had no history of using alcohol or drugs either. She was mostly described by those who knew her best as friendly, outgoing, vivacious, intelligent, and fun loving and she was said to have been the life of the party no matter where she was. At first glance Hannah lived a happy life and had no known enemies so it was really strange when, on a beautiful August day in 2008, she left her apartment in Manhattan to go for her usual jog but didn't return when she was supposed to. When she still hadn't shown back up or contacted anyone the next day, her friends called the police and reported her as missing. The investigators found nothing amiss or missing in her apartment and everything seemed to be there and in its rightful place. They found her MetroCard, her purse, cell phone, passport, and her wallet with all her cash and credit cards inside of it. As more days went by with no sign of or word from Hannah, the police started thinking the worst in that maybe she had been kidnapped or murdered when she went out for her jog that day. They finally launched a more intensive investigation and that's when things started getting extremely bizarre.

Nine days after she had initially vanished, and as her face was being splashed all over the news and other local media, along with it being posted everywhere on missing persons flyers, a man who was shopping at an Apple store in downtown Manhattan saw who he was one hundred percent sure was Hannah Upp. The witness said that he approached the woman and asked her if she was Hannah but the woman responded that he must be mistaken and he said she was seemingly in some sort of trance as she briskly walked away without looking back. After that initial sighting, it seemed like Hannah was spotted all over Manhattan and Soho at places like Starbucks, small shops and even a well-known sports bar in the area but it's like she was a ghost. Everyone who reported seeing her said she seemed like she was in some sort of trance or dazed state and whether or not the woman everyone was seeing was Hannah or not could never be determined because while the witnesses did always call the authorities, the woman would be gone by the time they arrived to check out the situation. Three weeks after Hannah's disappearance, in September of 2008, there would be an unusual discovery made in southern Manhattan.

It was September 16th and two men working at a ferry dock on the river near the statue of liberty saw something out of place bobbing around in the water and it didn't take long for them to realize it was a person. Some of the deckhands went out in the rescue boat, fully expecting to recover a dead body but they were in for a real shock when they got out there and realized that although she was bobbing face down in the water- perfectly still and inert- she was alive. They recognized her as the missing woman Hannah Upp right away and she was rushed to the hospital. Hannah was found to have a mild case of hypothermia; severe sunburn and she was severely dehydrated. Things would go from strange to downright bizarre as soon as she was lucid enough to speak and tell her story. First of all, when she spoke to the police she seemed genuinely surprised that three whole weeks had passed and that she had been gone for that long. She said the last thing that she remembered was leaving her apartment to go for a jog, and she had no memory at all of where she had been or what she had been doing in the interim. She had no recollection of shopping in Manhattan or Soho and she actually thought that someone was playing some sort of elaborate trick on her. She could not believe that she had been gone for three weeks. According to Hannah, as far as she knew, she had only been gone for about ten minutes- tops, and she told the New York Times, "I went from going for a run to being in the ambulance." In the hospital that first night Hannah was allegedly heard talking in her sleep and she kept saying something about being in a lighthouse, but when her mother asked her about it the next day, Hannah couldn't remember her dreams at all and had no idea what she had been talking about.

Hannah was questioned intensively and extensively and a whole slew of neurological tests were performed but when those tests turned up nothing unusual and there was nothing in her memory about what had actually happened to her or where she had been, the best theory the police and doctors could come up with what that she had been suffering from "dissociative fugue" which is also popularly called "Jason Bourne Syndrome." It's an extremely rare and poorly understood condition that causes a person suffering with it to lose awareness of their identity and other autobiographical information for any length of time, although they still maintain the ability to function and survive. During the episodes it's very common for the sufferer to create new identities and go off in unplanned trips. It can last for hours, days, weeks, months or even longer but it's almost always the result of some sort of powerful traumatic event in the person's life and strangely enough, neither Hannah nor her family and loved ones could think of what could have possibly been the cause for it for her. In fact, Hannah had NEVER had any sort of severe trauma inflicted on her in her whole life up to that point and that's what made the whole thing so incredibly bizarre- more so than it initially had seemed with everything that had happened leading up to that point. Psychiatrists even got Hannah's permission to hypnotize her to try and uncover what caused her to go into this fugue-like state because they were convinced that maybe she had dealt with a profound trauma but had possibly repressed it, but they never found anything like that in her subconscious mind either during the sessions. Regardless of what actually had happened and the fact there was no evidence of it having happened, Jason Bourne Syndrome was the best explanation at the time for what happened and Hannah wanted to just go back to living a normal life again. She tried to do just that but this isn't where the story ends- not by far!

Hannah moved to Maryland for a fresh start and went right back to teaching. At first she was loving her life and everything seemed perfectly fine and normal. However, in September of 2013, which was 5 years after her initial disappearance, Hannah Upp disappeared again. It started that time with the local police calling Hannah's mother to tell her that Hannah's wallet and cell phone were left lying abandoned inside of a wooded footpath in Kensington but there was no sign at all of where Hannah was or how the items had ended up there. She was missing for two days that time because she had made her way back to her house on her own after she said she woke up confused and lying in a shallow ditch next to an empty shopping cart. Once again she had no memory of where she had been from the moment she left her house until she woke up two days later. It didn't escape investigator's notice that both disappearances happened in September and somehow involved water- but there's still no known connection with those two details. However, she would disappear for a third time, again in September and again there would be some involvement with water that time too.

A year after the second disappearance, Hannah made the somewhat unusual move to the US Virgin Islands, in St. Thomas in the Caribbean, where she found a job again as a teacher. Once again everything seemed to be back to normal with Hannah and despite surviving two major hurricanes while living there, she seemed very happy with her life again. She even told her friends and family that she intended to stay there indefinitely because she loved it so much. Then, on September 17, 2017, Hannah casually told her roommates that she was going to work. She left that day as usual but ended up never coming back. When she didn't return by the next day and her friends found out she had never made it to work, they decided to go and look for her themselves. They found the clothes she had been wearing when she left the house folded neatly on the beach and her car keys lying nearby to where the clothes were. Her car was found in the parking lot and her purse was in there. Inside of her purse were her wallet, keys, cell phone and passport. Why had she removed her clothes and where had she gone without wearing any? No one knew what had happened to her but everyone was very worried wondering if she had stripped naked and gone swimming or snorkeling or something. The authorities were called in and a search was started that included boats and helicopters but there was no sign of Hannah anywhere. Morgues, hospitals, and homeless shelters all over the island were meticulously searched to try and find her but it was all to no avail. With St. Thomas being such a small island, everyone thought that eventually she would be found and quickly too but she never was. It seemed as though she had once again gone into some sort of amnesic fugue state, but if that's the case then she hasn't yet to this day snapped out of it. Hannah hasn't ever returned.

Just like with her first disappearance there were sightings of Hannah all over the place in the beginning of the investigation, and she was allegedly spotted all over the island. There was a report that she had been panhandling at a marina and someone else said they saw her hanging out around one of the homeless shelters. In every case of alleged sightings, Hannah was reported as being in that same dazed and trance-like state but none of the alleged sightings have led the authorities or her loved ones any closer to actually finding her or to finding out what happened to her. As is usually the case, none of the sightings of Hannah were ever officially able to be confirmed. Hannah Upp's story was featured in a documentary called Vanished in Paradise and her friends and family still cling to hope that she's alive out there but she might not know who she is. They believe she could be living a whole new life with no memory of who she really is or what happened to her. However, there's always the possibility that lurks in the backs of many of their minds that perhaps something sinister had happened to her and that she might not be alive at all. Her friends and family do their best to remain hopeful though that she simply forgot who she is and where she's from, and they've released a statement that said, "We've done all the physical searching that I think we can do, other than having her posters put up everywhere. That's going to be the only way, hopefully, if she sees one of them, if she's in her fugue state, it would at least get her to the point where she realizes something's wrong and she goes to get help. That's what we're hoping for. We have no way of knowing the length of time Hannah's condition and journey may fill. We are in this for the long haul."

So, what happened to Hannah Upp? How could someone go missing for weeks on end with no memory of where they had been or how they had gotten where they had ended up? Is there something more sinister at play here than just a very rare medical condition- an anomaly? If I'm being honest, this case had me thinking of all of the missing college aged young men who go out for a night of partying or are otherwise out late at night and they end up missing, only to be found in nearby water sources they had no business being near in the first place. A lot of those cases are mysterious and suspicious and I will be discussing some of them here in this book. I have one theory for what's happening there that could fit here, and we will talk about that when we get to those cases but for Hannah I've been thinking of something somewhat different. It's possible, if we are thinking in terms of the supernatural and otherworldly, that something was happening to Hannah that had something to do with some otherworldly entity that needed her for something. Perhaps the first two disappearances were test runs for the entities but they failed and needed to make sure they succeeded in getting her to where they needed her to be. Listen, not all abductions are straight and to the point with the entity coming into your bedroom at night and stealing you away to run some medical tests and experiments for a little while. Sometimes they have different methods and I believe, if this wasn't a case of some medical anomaly, then it was most likely an otherworldly entity that was entrancing Hannah to test run, finally abducting her. She's more than likely out there somewhere, whether it be in the cosmos or under the ocean, which by the way is where some people think she ended up, only they think she drowned after stripping and walking into the water herself. I believe she was entranced and compelled to do so and that she is underwater in a base, like so many others who go missing under similarly bizarre circumstances. As always I hope that Hannah's found or returns one day, even though more than likely she never will. I always remind people that we have no idea what's really going on underneath our oceans and in the depths of the seas on our planet and there's really no kind of coincidence I could or would ever be able to believe in where you could convince me that all of the strange sightings of lights in the water and reports of people being abducted and taken to small and enclosed cities under the sea, have nothing to do with any of these bizarre disappearances, Hannah's included.

I have to be honest here guys, I couldn't help but keep thinking about the missing college aged men who have been going missing all over the United States and Canada while out partying and randomly disappearing without a trace or without being caught on any sort of surveillance footage and then ending up in nearby water sources they had no business being anywhere near. You guys have asked me to do a video on whether or not there were women who it happened to as well but despite my many attempts at finding cases of females enduring the same types of tragedies, I couldn't find anything like that. Hannah's case makes me wonder if maybe that's because no one has connected the cases yet. Is there a significance of all of her disappearances happening in September or of the water sources that seem to be connected with all three of them? No one knows and as of when I am writing this script, there's been no updates or new information on whatever happened to Hannah Upp.

CHAPTER EIGHT

WILLIAM ROACH

Everyone who knew William Roach called him Bill. Bill has been missing for more than thirty years now and it's believed a curse from a witch is what led to his demise.

William "Bill" Roach was a twenty five year old university student when he went missing in Armidale, Northern Tablelands, New South Wales, Australia, back on New Year's Eve in 1993. The police still have no idea what happened to him but at the time of his disappearance, he was believed to have been living with his girlfriend who described herself as being a practicing witch. There is definitely a possibility that some kind of black magic or curse is directly involved here in this case. Prior to his disappearance, he went to a "secret ceremony" for witches where magic mushrooms were known to grow. While he was there, the attendees asked him to walk across a stream by only touching the stones; however, he disobeyed and jumped right into the water. His disobedience caused one of the witches to allegedly put a "death curse" on him and shortly after the ceremony, he went missing. Could this all be just a coincidence? I'll tell you right now it's never a coincidence and I don't believe in them when it comes to things like this anyway. There's no way it all just happened to work out this way.

It's been reported that William really believed he was the victim of this death curse. Just like in the Christopher case incident, which I mention in multiple books I've written, it really affected him. New England Police District Commander Detective Superintendent

Steve Laksa stated that the angle of witchcraft was being pursued, although they were following up on several other angles such as Roach possibly being part of a drug organization. Let me just stop here for a minute... it's "being pursued"? How in the world do you even begin to pursue something you would never in a million years be able to prove one way or another? Superintendent Laksa noted that William probably "fell into harm's way" and asked anyone who was involved with the drug trade in Armidale back in 1993 to reach out to authorities. While he wouldn't confirm or deny whether witchcraft was connected to the drug investigation, he did say, "There are a number of persons or interests from varying groups." So, he wants people "from the drug trade" to come forward and admit involvement in illegal activities? OK, sure. So, did one of the witches at the ceremony really put a "death curse" on William Roach for something as small as messing up their ceremony? Was it all about him trying to have some fun with it and not following the directions for crossing the stream, or was he a victim of foul play? Or is there something else altogether going on here which just hasn't been put together yet?

William's body has never been discovered and without any human remains, it's hard to know for sure what exactly happened to him. It's been so long and still no closure for his loved ones or any definitive answers at all but hopefully the one million dollar reward that's being offered for any information regarding the disappearance will change that. I know that many of you reading this probably think that real witches, curses, and death spells are the things of fiction novels and sub-par horror films but that isn't the case at all. There are many worlds and realms all around us that interact with us in many ways on a daily basis, we are just too closed off to see and realize it. However, there are some people who practice the art of witchcraft who have no qualms with cursing someone over the smallest thing or for any reason at all. With black magick- and I use that term loosely and only for lack of something better- the more harm you do the more you receive as far as power. This is a hard pill to swallow for most people but I am telling you from my own experience how true it is. You can do what you like with the information I'm providing but at the end of the day a man is missing and has left behind loved ones and people who still grieve for him. Being that there was a self-proclaimed witch involved here and the fact that William himself really thought a death curse had been put on him, even though there's relatively no information out there about what made him so sure this was the case, besides that one of the witches at the ceremony said it, that sometimes is enough itself to bring a curse to life. Please be careful when playing with the occult and practicing magick, as often the price we pay for such power is our humanity. I hope one day that William's grieving loved ones find peace and I hope the witch who cursed him has it come back to her tenfold.

CHAPTER NINE

RANDY DOYLE PARSCALE JR.

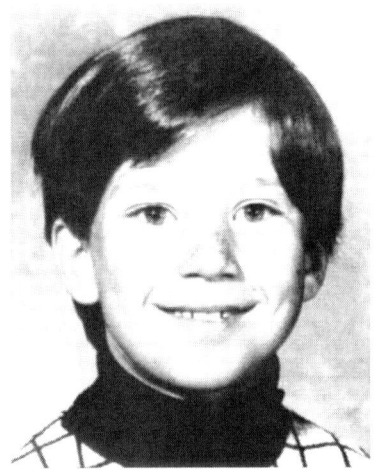

Randy Doyle Parscale Jr. was born on April January 13, 1969, to parents Randy Sr and Peggy Parscale, now Foley. They divorced shortly after he was born. Randy Jr was raised by his father and stepmother, Naomi, on 31st street in Tucson, Arizona and attended the third grade at Roberts Elementary School. Randy Jr was described as loving and affectionate and it's said he liked to tell people he was "strong like the Incredible Hulk." According to his stepmother Naomi, he was a bit of a loner and liked to do things by himself and on his own. He loved to make his schoolmates laugh and was unofficially voted the "Second cutest guy" in his third grade class. He had a lot of trouble in school as far as not only academic work but his behavior as well, though it's said he was actively working very hard to improve both of those things. At the time of his disappearance Randy Jr was about to be named Citizen of the Week at his school. This was a very high honor among third graders because it required nine whole and straight weeks of positive behavior and no reprimands. Unfortunately, Randy was never able to see himself named because he disappeared before it happened.

On Saturday, April 7th, 1979, ten year old Randy, along with his father, grandfather, two siblings and an uncle visited a place called Peppersauce Canyon, a few miles northeast or Oracle in the Santa Catalina Mountains. The family spent the day together and were rock collecting when Randy Jr grew tired of the activity and didn't want to do it anymore. Eventually he and his eleven year old brother Robert approached their grandfather Walter Guthrie, who also wasn't participating and was relaxing in the shade off to the side of the group, if they could go on a short hike together instead. Walter said that they could but that they needed to be careful. Randy hadn't ever been on a hike before but the boy's uncle said he would go with them while Randy's father and sister stayed behind with Walter. The spot where they chose to climb was treacherous to say the least. It was full of loose rocks and cacti and hidden among the scrub oak and pines were shin diggers. Robbie got some thorns in his feet and when his uncle stopped to help him out, Randy became impatient while waiting for them to be ready to continue on. Eventually Randy took off on his own, racing up the mountain as his brother and uncle yelled for him to stop and wait for them. He didn't listen to them though and kept making his way up the side as fast as he could. That was the last anyone ever saw of him.

His uncle rounded the same bend moments later but there was no sign of Randy and no clue as to where he could have gone. Randy was last seen approximately two hundred yards away from a campground at the canyon's mouth alongside the old Mount Lemmon highway. As soon as word that Randy was missing reached his stepmother Naomi, she along with Randy's grandmothers and his mother, rushed as fast as they could to the campground. As they neared the campground they didn't think too much about the black Ford Mustang speeding by them, seemingly not caring about the speed limit or other drivers on the road. They were too concerned with Randy and his whereabouts. They merely thought the man should slow down because he was going far too fast for the conditions of the road at the time. Later it would be found out that Randy was last seen having a conversation with the driver of that vehicle and it was said that the man had been carrying some camping equipment. A witness came forward who said they had seen Randy Jr at around 5:30 that evening and that he appeared to be hitchhiking. If the boy seen was Randy then he was heading into the mountain and not away from it but it's never been confirmed one way or another if the boy seen was Randy or not. Search and Rescue included about six dozen people, some of whom were on horseback and tracker dogs, all searching for six straight days for Randy. They meticulously searched and researched the areas where he was last seen, last allegedly seen and last known to be, plus all of the surrounding areas to those places. They searched in caves and old mine shafts and performed aerial searches but it was all to no avail.

Searchers found some footprints that led to a main road but they abruptly stopped which led them to believe whoever they belonged to had gotten into a vehicle and was driven off. Both the police and Randy's father were skeptical at best as to whether the footprints belonged to the boy. A man named Chuck McHugh coordinated the search and rescue efforts for Randy said of the footprints, "He was wearing a shoe with a large tread pattern and exaggerated waves from side to side" and while the footprints somewhat matched that pattern specifically, it's said that at least one other member of the search party had been wearing sneakers with a very similar tread pattern on them and the tracks could have very well belonged to that person as well. Though the temperature dropped into the mid-forties, the police were confident that Randy could have survived on his own for a few days, provided he was still there and uninjured, due to the many water sources and areas in the canyon. A few days after the searches initially began, the weather took a turn for the worse when snow and fifty five mph winds came rolling through the canyon. This greatly impacted the search and temperatures dropped into the low thirties. Tracking dogs that were specifically trained to search in the wilderness were brought in and utilized as well and their handler said that if Randy had still been in the canyon then those dogs would have definitely found him, one way or another. They didn't find him and no one ever has.

After five and a half days of searching and with no

new leads and the weather getting worse and worse as the days ticked by, the police reluctantly called off the search for the ten year old boy. The search up to that point had cost around fifty thousand dollars and once it was called off the case was officially reassigned and handed over to Detective Tom Rankin of the Pinal County Sheriff's Department. The search was so grueling and intense that on the fifth day, a man named Manuel M. Navarro, who was just forty nine years old, died of a heart attack while helping to look for Randy Jr. Randy's family believe he was abducted from the canyon and although he had been known to run away before, there were no signs at that time that he was unhappy or wanting to run away again. There was only one real clue that even had the possibility of helping everyone learn what could have possibly happened to Randy. During the search a man came forward and told authorities that Randy had stopped at his campground on the night he had disappeared. All he managed to say was that it had been sometime that night, just as it started to get cooler outside. However, the man seemingly vanished himself and left the area before he could be properly interviewed. According to the newspaper, The Tucson Citizen, "police had a license plate number for the camper that was issued in Arizona but the car for which the license was issued turned up in a wrecking yard in California." They were never able to locate the camper. In early May of 1979, the police conducted another search for Randy due to a hunter coming forward and reporting previously unknown and extremely treacherous terrain at Peppersauce Canyon. The search was unsuccessful and despite a woman and her two children coming forward at that time and stating that they had seen Randy after he had been reported as missing, nothing more came from that witness and lead either. They were so desperate the police even tried to use psychics on numerous occasions but were unsuccessful there too. All of them stated that Randy wasn't alive anymore but then they all gave different locations for where his body was allegedly located. No remains were ever found in any of the locations given by the psychics, or anywhere else for that matter.

A dollar bill surfaced with writing on it that claimed to be that of Randy Parscale Jr's, stating that he was alive and well and living in Phoenix Arizona. It stated "help me" along with the other information but the authorities weren't ever able to track down where it had come from or who wrote on it. It's unknown whether or not it was Randy but most people think it's highly unlikely given how easy it is for someone to pick up a dollar bill and write whatever they want on it before sending it back out into circulation. In 1989 Randy's father received information that someone who fit Randy's description was using his social security number and working at a construction site in Phoenix, Arizona but by the time he drove out there to investigate, the man was no longer employed there. The police picked up the investigation into that lead but were also never able to locate the man. On the 21st anniversary of his disappearance, Randy's mother, and sister, along with many other family members, friends and loved ones, went to the Children's Memorial Park in Tucson to bid a final farewell to him. They said they needed to admit it was finally time to move on. Randy's sister Pam Brume, who was thirty three years old at the time of the memorial service, told authorities that right before it was to be held, a former Salvation Army counselor told her that Randy's disappearance had become a campsite and fireside legend. The story told is that of a boy who vanished into thin air while walking among the trees of the vast forest and who disappeared in the blink of an eye, never to be seen or heard from again. The counselor said that while they were telling the story, the young campers "observed a unique butterfly shape in a clearing near the camp and started calling Randy the Butterfly Boy." From the moment they saw the butterfly and gave Randy that nickname, the story became a warning for them to never wander off alone and the legend brought a sense of peace and comfort to his biological mother and sister.

The last interview his mother gave was on National Missing Children's Day in May of 2010 but his father continued actively searching for his son. He believes Randy was abducted and taken out of the canyon the same day he went missing. Unfortunately, Randy Parscale Sr passed away in June of 2003, never having found out what happened to his beloved eldest son. He was 59 years old. Much of the rest of his family still live in and around the Tucson area in Arizona. Many theories and a lot of speculation had sprung up around this case throughout the years but the general consensus is that Randy was abducted. After all, the trackers were adamant the trained dogs would have definitely found him had he still been in or near the canyon. Randy Parscale Jr went missing from Oracle Arizona and his disappearance is ruled a non-family abduction. He is a Caucasian male who weighed approximately seventy pounds and stood at four foot, six inches tall at the time of his disappearance. He was born on January 13th, 1969, and would have turned fifty four years old this year. He was last seen wearing a long sleeved red and green striped shirt, an olive green hunter's vest or jacket and blue jeans. He also wore shoes with a bulls-eye pattern on the soles. He suffers from asthma and has brown hair and blue eyes.

So here we have yet another case where dogs don't seem to want to do their jobs or where they seemingly can't for some reason and the sudden onset of inclement weather during an extensive search. I mention it time and time again, particularly in my book Missing: The Fae Theory, that whatever is out there- and believe me it's many things- has a power and ability to control search efforts and steer the finding of any clues or the gaining of any knowledge into these disappearances away from the truth. Maybe we just aren't prepared to know what's really happening out there, meaning human beings as a whole. Randy was an exceptional kid and that's another fact that meets the standard in these types of cases. When it comes to disappearances in the wilderness, the possibilities are endless, but if something is out there abducting human beings for whatever reason, and if it is really responsible for all of the walls put up between finding the truth about what happened to the person involved, then it has got to be something supernatural or otherworldly. I say that at the risk of sounding like a broken record because it doesn't compute for me that people don't automatically go to this type of explanation. The good news is that the entities and creatures lurking out there aren't always wanting to harm the people they take, regardless of if they actually do or not. The butterfly legend was particularly interesting to me and made me think that maybe this child had that something special that seems to attract the fae like bees to honey. Children are very innocent, even at that age, and they are much more open to the otherworldly than we are as adults, for the most part. It's possible that this boy was taken by the fae folk and that he was able, with as exceptional as he was, to put the idea of him into the other children's heads as he sent the butterfly as a messenger. "I'm here. I'm alright." I almost never prefer to wrap these disappearances up in neat little packages but for me, with the type of work that I do, it's glaringly obvious that he could have been taken by the fae and that he's okay. After all, it's a heck of a lot better than having to consider the alternative involving the Ford Mustang- isn't it?

EXCERPT
MIDNIGHT VISITORS

It Followed Me Home

As I write this, my hands are still trembling from the encounter I had last night. It was around midnight, and I was walking back from a friend's place. The streets were deserted, and an eerie silence enveloped the neighborhood. That's when I heard it — a faint, almost hesitant, knocking. Turning around, I saw a small figure standing at the corner of the street.

The child, couldn't have been more than ten, was dressed in an outdated manner, like something out of a mid-20th-century photograph. But it was their eyes that sent a chill down my spine — pitch black, with no trace of white. It felt like staring into a void. "Can you help me?" the child asked in a monotone voice. Their words seemed rehearsed, unnatural.

I felt a compulsion to help, yet every instinct screamed at me to run. The air around us grew colder, and a suffocating sense of dread enveloped me. "I... I need to get home," I stammered, backing away. The child's expression never changed, but their eyes seemed to grow darker, if that were even possible.

I turned and ran, not daring to look back. The sound of my heart pounding in my ears was louder than my footsteps. When I finally reached home, I slammed the door shut and leaned against it, gasping for breath. I don't know who or what that child was, but their haunting black eyes and eerie presence have been etched into my mind, a chilling reminder of the night I encountered something inexplicable.

The encounter with the black-eyed child was far from over. That same night, after I had calmed down and convinced myself it was just a figment of my overactive imagination, I heard it again — a soft, persistent knocking at my front door. My heart froze. It couldn't be, I thought.

With a sense of dread overwhelming me, I approached the door. The knocking continued, rhythmic and insistent. I peered through the peephole, and there the child stood, their face emotionless, those deep, black eyes staring right back at me as if they could see through the door.

I couldn't understand how they had found where I lived. The child spoke again, their voice a haunting whisper, "Please, let me in. I'm lost and it's cold." Every fiber of my being screamed against opening the door. The air in my house felt thick, charged with a palpable sense of fear.

I backed away from the door, unable to break eye contact with the figure through the peephole. The child's expression never changed, but their eyes seemed to grow more intense, more compelling. I whispered, "I can't help you," my voice barely audible.

The knocking ceased abruptly, leaving behind a silence that felt almost suffocating. I watched for several minutes, but the child didn't move. They just stood there, staring. Then, as suddenly as they had appeared, they turned and vanished into the night.

I didn't sleep that night, nor many nights after. The image of the black-eyed child at my doorstep haunted me, a chilling reminder of an encounter that defied explanation and left me questioning the very nature of what I had seen.

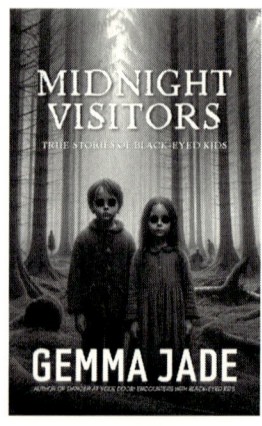

Midnight Visitors: True Stories of Black-Eyed Kids

EXCERPT 2
CAMPFIRE STORIES: ENCOUNTERS IN THE WOODS

A Mysterious Encounter in the Forest

It was in the late 2000s, during a phase of my mid-twenties when life seemed to be a relentless wave of responsibilities and deadlines. I was working a demanding corporate job at a family-owned company, a position I had taken up right after graduating from high school. Simultaneously, I was pursuing further education to enhance my prospects within the company. The combined pressure of work and studies was immense, and at that time, it felt like the heaviest burden I had ever shouldered.

In search of solace and a brief escape from the clutches of my everyday life, I planned a weekend camping trip. The destination was a familiar one – a dense, sprawling forest that I had visited countless times since childhood. There was something about the woods, with their towering trees and serene silence, that always brought me peace. This trip, I hoped, would provide the much-needed mental respite.

I arrived at the forest as the sun began its descent, painting the sky in hues of orange and purple. My camper found its usual spot at the edge of the woods. The forest's interior was too dense, the trails too narrow for vehicles. I didn't mind the extra effort of setting up a tent; in fact, the ritual was part of the charm.

My tent was a sturdy, spacious one, comfortably accommodating one person. Setting it up was second nature to me, a skill honed over years of frequent camping. As darkness enveloped the forest, I managed to get my tent pitched just in time. The only source of light now was the flickering fire I had kindled, its warm glow a comforting presence in the enveloping darkness.

Dinner was a simple affair – canned food heated over the fire. There's something about eating in the wilderness that makes even the most mundane meal seem like a feast. As I ate, I felt the stress and noise of my regular life fading away, replaced by the tranquility of the forest.

After dinner, an unusual impulse struck me. Despite never having ventured into the woods at night, I suddenly felt an overpowering urge to explore. A trail to my left, which I hadn't noticed earlier, seemed to beckon me. Curiosity overcame caution, and with my flashlight in hand, I set off into the night.

The trail was narrow, winding through thick undergrowth and ancient trees. At first, the adventure felt exhilarating, a spontaneous deviation from my usually planned life. However, about ten minutes into my walk, the atmosphere changed. The air seemed charged, electric, and I felt a prickling sensation on my skin, as if I had walked into an unseen web.

Panic set in swiftly and without warning. My heart raced, my breathing became erratic, and a sense of dread enveloped me. I realized I was experiencing a panic attack, something I had never encountered before. The forest, once a source of peace, now felt like an oppressive, alien world.

I found solace under a large tree, its massive trunk and sprawling roots offering a sense of protection. As I sat there, trying to steady my breathing, I noticed something peculiar – a bright pink light flickering in the distance. It wasn't the warm glow of a campfire but something otherworldly, something I had never seen before in all my years of camping.

Driven by a mix of curiosity and an inexplicable sense of calm that replaced my panic, I approached the light. As I drew closer, I realized it was unlike anything natural. It resembled a giant, floating orb, about my height, with edges that undulated like waves. Inside the orb was a scene of bright colors and daylight, a stark contrast to the night around me.

I could see figures in the distance within this illuminated sphere, their gestures inviting. They seemed to be beckoning me, their mouths moving as if calling out, though no sound reached my ears. I walked around the orb, inspecting it from all angles, only to find the forest continued uninterrupted behind it. This realization that the orb was some kind of portal or window to another world sent a shiver down my spine.

As I stood there, mesmerized, the light began to flicker erratically. The figures' expressions transformed from welcoming to menacing, their faces distorting into grotesque forms. Human features twisted into demonic visages, then back again, in a horrifying dance. The once inviting portal now seemed a gateway to a nightmarish realm.

Fear gripped me, and I stumbled backward, away from the changing scene. The orb's light dimmed, and as it did, the opening seemed to contract, the gateway closing. I turned and ran back to my camp, my mind racing with terror and confusion.

Whispers filled the air around me as I fled, not the whispers of humans, but sounds of anguish and despair, like the cries of tormented souls. They seemed to emanate from the very air, following me as I sprinted through the dark forest.

Back at my campsite, I was unable to find peace. Sleep was an impossibility; my mind was a tumult of fear and disbelief. I lay in my tent, the events replaying in my mind. Had I stumbled upon a portal to another dimension? My knowledge of such concepts was limited to science fiction and horror movies – they weren't topics discussed openly in the early nineties.

Hours passed, and nature's call forced me out of my tent. As I ventured a short distance into the woods for privacy, I heard rustling nearby. It sounded large, and the fear that had ebbed away came rushing back. I turned slowly, half expecting to see a wild animal.

Instead, I was confronted by a man. He was of average height, with a plain appearance that was almost uncanny in its ordinariness. He wore simple clothes – jeans, a white t-shirt, and sturdy boots. His hair and eyes were a nondescript brown, his skin neither pale nor tanned. He was, in every aspect, remarkably unremarkable.

His demeanor was odd; his arms raised in a mock surrender, a playful smirk on his lips. He took a step towards me, and I instinctively stepped back. His casual lean against a tree did little to ease my apprehension.

Then, he spoke, his voice devoid of any accent, as ordinary as his appearance. He commented on my earlier panic, as if he had read my mind. My thoughts turned to the portal, and he casually mentioned it, confirming my suspicion that he was no ordinary man.

He extended an invitation, a chance to explore the world beyond the portal, the same world the figures had been trying to lure me into. My refusal was immediate. His reaction was startling – his features twisted into a demonic visage, mirroring the transformations I had witnessed in the orb.

I cursed and turned to run, but a sound stopped me – a howl, primal and wild, coming from where the man had stood. When I looked back, he was gone, leaving only a faint trace of the pink light.

I didn't linger to investigate. Packing my belongings, I left the woods, driven by an overwhelming need to escape. The experience haunted me, initially dismissed as a mental breakdown. But in the years that followed, as I delved into research and heard of similar encounters, my perspective shifted.

I came to believe that I had encountered a thin veil between our world and another, possibly a glimpse into a hellish dimension. The ordinary man, I now suspect, was a demonic entity, perhaps even the devil, attempting to claim my soul.

The experience, though initially terrifying, became a turning point in my life. It led me to reconsider my priorities and values. I returned to the woods eventually, but the encounter remains a profound, unexplained chapter in my life – a reminder of the mysteries that lie beyond the veil of our understanding.

Read more
CAMPFIRE STORIES: ENCOUNTERS IN THE WOODS

CHAPTER TEN

KAREN SYKES

Of course, there are times when someone who has mysteriously disappeared does eventually show up again, oftentimes with a very bizarre or confusing story, and then there are times when a body is found, deceased. However, that doesn't always mean that the many questions get answered or that the riddle of what happened to them in the first place is solved. On June 14, 2018, a seventy year old woman named Karen Sykes went hiking with her boyfriend Greg Johnston in the Owyhigh Lakes area of Mount Rainier National Park. Despite her age, Karen was in excellent shape and in good health. She was also a very experienced hiker and climber. She had actually written several books and articles about those things and she also had her own hiking blog. Karen Sykes was an expert on hiking and climbing if ever there was one, and she knew the trails specifically at Mount Rainier very well. The reason Karen and Greg were out there hiking on that day was because she was looking to write an article about it and when they reached about five thousand feet, she told him she was going on ahead to do some scouting but that she would be right back. Now keep in mind the weather was clear and they had been on a stretch of well-worn and highly traveled trail that they had both been on many times before, but still and all, Karen never came back. Of course, once it had been more than a few minutes, her boyfriend decided to go and look for her but he wasn't really concerned and probably thought she had just been taking it slow or perhaps that she was merely taking in the scenery or something. What I mean to say is, I highly doubt that he was worried right away.

When he couldn't find her anywhere and when his screaming her name throughout the trail and the surrounding area turned up no sign of her, he became concerned and contacted the authorities. A search was immediately launched using six ground crews, two dog teams and an aircraft but Karen still wasn't found. It was seen as very bizarre from the very beginning because of how experienced Karen was and just because of who she was in general, not to mention how easy the trail was and how nice the weather had been. Nothing about her disappearance made any sense. No one could understand how someone so seasoned and professional could become so very lost and delineated on a trail she had been on hundreds of times before and with how much experience she had and all in just a matter of a few minutes.

The search continued for several days but on the third day, three days after she disappeared, her body was found under even more mysterious circumstances. She was discovered up steep, rugged terrain that was very far off from the trail that she had originally been on in the first place and there was no known reason for her to have gone so far or been there at all. It was also an area that's very difficult to get to and no one could understand why or how she managed to become so turned around or get so far off the trail to have ended up there in the first place. Adding to the mystery, a clear cause of death couldn't be determined and her body had no signs of any injuries at all. The coroner finally concluded that she had died from a mixture of hypothermia and a heart condition. That was also highly suspicious and strange. Karen had been dressed well for the occasion and for the weather and she was described by friends, family and others who knew her best as being very physically fit for her age. She told her boyfriend she would be back in just a minute or two so no one can figure out why she went so far off the trail or why she didn't just scout for the aforementioned minute or two and return to him like she said she would. It didn't make any sense back then and it still doesn't now. What in the world could this woman have seen that would have made her so thoroughly not only leave the area she was in and knew so well, but to have her wandering so far off and into an area that was extremely hard to get to and that she had no business being in? Not to mention the hypothermia! She was well dressed for the weather by all accounts.

To me it sounds like she was either lured away by something or that she was overcome with what I see so much happening in the wilderness all too often, and that's the overwhelming dizziness and confusion people who wander off alone in the woods always claim to have felt right before they went missing. Well, in speaking of those who make it back anyway. She made it all the way up that treacherous and steep ridge just to what? Just to die mysteriously? There had to have been a reason she was there in the first place but without more information it's impossible to know and the case remains a tragic mystery to this day, just like so many others. I couldn't help but notice how exceptional Karen was as a person but also how exceptional she was in her field of expertise. She was someone who stood out in a crowd and when I was reading through her case when deciding which to include here in this book, I couldn't help but draw a connection from her case to so many of the others I've reviewed through the course of my professional career. Exceptional people who are out doing what they love to do or who are out in the wilderness or somewhere doing their job and then they're gone in the blink of an eye with no evidence left behind and no sense to be made about what actually happened to them. When I talk about the information I've gathered about many different races of otherworldly entities who roam the woods cloaked or who hover above the woodlands of our world in vehicles or crafts that are cloaked as well and how they could be the cause for these types of abductions, I often wonder what their intent is with us or with those who they choose to take.

    I don't think they're experimenting on the humans

they take in a torturous sort of way but I do believe an experiment is absolutely what they're running with these people. I've seen so many cases, time after time, where someone makes it out of the woods alive but tells a story about how they were suddenly overwhelmed with confusion and they feel nauseous and dizzy suddenly and seemingly out of nowhere- I think that they were targeted to be the next victims of these otherworldly entities but they were fortunate enough to somehow escape the clutches of their otherworldly abductors. Why are they taking them is the question you're probably asking and honestly that depends on the entity itself and what its motives are but I've come to at least one conclusion which I've briefly mentioned in this book already. I believe they are trying to start a "new Earth" so to speak, where human beings don't have as much freedom and autonomy but where they live in peace and harmony with one another and with nature, as many extraterrestrial and interdimensional beings do and believe that's how we were meant to live here from the beginning. Think of Lemuria or Atlantis- I believe they're being taken to a place like that where they either don't have the memory of their lives here or they aren't able to put up much of a fight because they understand that their body won't cross through the portal alive again. Meaning, I believe this is why so many people turn up deceased under incredibly strange and unexplainable circumstances, like Karen Sykes.

Did she accidentally cross through a portal to another dimension? It's possible but I believe she might have been lured by some otherworldly entity or creature that needed her area of expertise and maybe she would rather have risked the return trip home than stay wherever she was brought to for the remainder of her life. I also wonder in cases like this if perhaps it really is a benevolent race of beings that are orchestrating all of this and maybe sometimes the trip back through the portal or whatever it was that was used to take the person in the first place inadvertently has the effect of killing the person and, more than likely, landing them in some random area of the wilderness they had no business ever being at that time. This could be why so many people are found deceased miles away from where they go missing, with no rhyme or reason as to how they got there or why they would have ended up there in the first place.

CHAPTER ELEVEN

DEORR KUNZ JR.

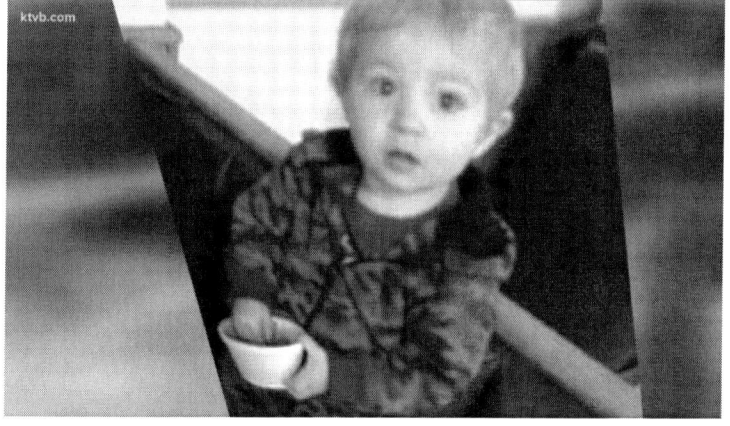

On July 10, 2015, Jessica Mitchell and her fiancé Vernal DeOrr Kunz Sr. of Idaho Falls, Idaho decided to take a spontaneous camping trip at the Timber Creek Campground in the Salmon-Challis National Forest in Lemhi County, Idaho. They brought along Jessica's grandfather, Robert Walton, his friend Isaac Reinwand, and their two year old son DeOrr Jr. By all accounts it was meant to be a fun and exciting trip and as they made their way to the destination, everyone was in really high spirits. The group spent some time planning the trip and packing everything they would need to have a good time together. Little DeOrr was especially excited, being only two years old, and couldn't wait to get to the campsite so he could run around and spend some time with his family. The trip hadn't been planned at all beforehand and was seen by everyone as an exciting impromptu adventure. However, and be that as it may, everyone involved was about to take a very dark detour down a path of mystery, accusations, and intrigue that, when it was all said and done, would be left as one of the most bizarre and enduring mysteries of our modern time.

The drive to the campground took two hours and they arrived in the early afternoon and once the group arrived at the remote and mountainous campsite, they set up their camper trailer and then spent some time exploring the campground. DeOrr's parents took him for a little ride of the truck he had brought with him and by all accounts the toddler was enjoying the fresh air and sunshine as much as everyone else was. As the sun began to set, the group roasted marshmallows on the fire. DeOrr's parents put him to bed in the tent and read him a bedtime story. Once he was asleep they went and joined Issac and Robert by the fire again to converse and enjoy the nighttime in such a gorgeous and scenic environment. On the second day of the trip, after waking up early and having some breakfast, the group decided to go fishing. They packed all of their gear up and set out for a nearby creek. Jessica and Vernal held their son's hand as they walked along the creek together and DeOrr played in the water. They caught some fish and returned to the campsite to fry them up for lunch. After lunch DeOrr was put down for a nap in his tent and immediately after he woke up is where is where the details begin to get murky. Everything is alleged and depending upon who you believe and missing persons and mysteries takes no stance one way or another and is accusing no one of doing anything untoward or of engaging in any criminal behavior. We are only looking for the truth and reporting the facts as best as we can find them.

When Jessica and Vernal decided to go for a walk, Isaac was already down by the creek fishing again. DeOrr was playing nearby to where his great grandfather was sitting in a chair and Jessica and Vernal yelled to him that they wanted him to watch DeOrr for them so they could go down to the creek and get some fishing in themselves. Depending on which source you get your information from, Robert Walton either agreed to watch the little boy and gave him some candy or he was inside the camper trailer with the door open and afterwards said he hadn't even known he was supposed to be watching the child to begin with. However, most sources agree that he was outside and had offered DeOrr some candy to get him to stay with him so his parents could spend some time together. About ten minutes later Vernal and Jessica came back to get DeOrr because they wanted to show him the minnows in the water at the creek but the toddler was nowhere in sight and Jessica's grandfather had no idea where he'd gone off to. Everyone fanned out and looked for the little boy and called his name but those calls repeatedly went unanswered and there was no sign of him anywhere. The parents asked nearby campers if they'd seen him but no one had. After about twenty minutes of searching on their own the family realized they needed professional help and called the authorities. A massive search operation was launched to find the two year old.

The search teams included law enforcement personnel, search and rescue professionals and volunteers. The operation began in the area around the campsite, where DeOrr Jr was last seen and was then expanded to cover a very large area of the campground itself. Search teams used a wide variety of equipment and methodically searched every inch of the large area designated to them- despite no one really believing a toddler could get very far in such a short amount of time in such hazardous and treacherous terrain. Search dogs, drones, and helicopters were used in the searches and searchers looked around on foot, on horseback and they also utilized ATVs. The search for DeOrr was challenging because of the treacherous terrain and the dense forest that surrounded the campground itself. In the end no stone was left unturned but no trace of DeOrr was ever found. The search teams did everything they could to navigate the steep terrain and through the thick vegetation, searching for any sign or inkling of the boy or what happened to him. The weather also posed a challenge to the search teams as the temperatures were high and the air was dry- that made it very difficult for search dogs to track and intermittent thunderstorms and other inclement weather caused many difficulties and unforeseen challenges for the search and rescue teams and authorities who were all desperate to find the little boy alive and unharmed. The rugged terrain and denseness of the forest made it hard for everyone to maintain communication within the teams as well. The heat and dry air made it so the dogs needed constant breaks so as not to become dehydrated and the search teams had to physically collect and carry water and other supplies to one another and to the canines, which caused even more logistical problems throughout the searches too.

The search for DeOrr was a massive undertaking and the authorities credit the volunteers that came in from all over the country as well as from local areas. Local church groups, search and rescue groups and all sorts of volunteers from all walks and areas of life showed up to Lemhi County to assist them but when everything was all said and done there was never even a single trace of the toddler that was found. The community rallied around the family and offered prayers and emotional support and many more resources to all of them. The community also played a vital role in getting the information about the disappearance out there to the masses by spreading the word on social media and putting up his missing person poster wherever it was they were from- and they were from all over the country by that point. The sheer number of people who showed up to try and help in any way they could for this little boy and his family is unlike anything the family or local law enforcement had ever seen before and the whole country was holding their breath, praying that DeOrr Kunz Jr would be found safe and unharmed and returned to his family.

All of the efforts from volunteers helped to make sure that the disappearance remained in the public eye which generated countless leads and tips for investigators to follow up with. While the community's involvement was critical in helping the search and in keeping his face front and center in the media, it also presented its own set of problems. The false leads and rumors that were generated because of such massive coverage cost the investigators precious time they could have been doing something worthwhile and the sheer volume of people were very hard to maintain during the actual searchers as they were responsible for making sure every single person searching or even handing out information stayed safe while doing so. The rumors were rampant on social media and authorities had to sift through that sort of information as well as whatever good tips and leads came in. In the end and after weeks of searching, the authorities were unable to find DeOrr and the search operations were eventually called off completely. The search operation for DeOrr Kunz Jr was one of the most extensive and expensive in the history of Idaho but despite it all, he has never been found and the mystery of what happened to him still endures to this day.

One of the most confusing aspects of the case for outsiders is the presence of several suspects who have been linked to DeOrr's disappearance being connected to him- as in they are members of his own family. Jessica and Vernal, DeOrr's parents, have been suspects almost from day one in this case and investigators say that they gave numerous conflicting statements and both failed several polygraph tests. They've given conflicting accounts of what happened the day he disappeared and in the hours leading up to the disappearance as well. One example is that Vernal initially claimed that he had taken DeOrr to a store near the campground while Jessica stated that at that same time, she had been with the toddler at the campsite. Another thing that's raised suspicions and that investigators have pointed out is Vernal's alleged history of domestic violence and the couple's alleged history of drug abuse. They were reportedly, according to investigators, allegedly, under the influence of some sort of substance the day DeOrr went missing. The couple has had to constantly deny having any involvement in their son's disappearance and they've consistently denied that they know what happened to him that day, going so far as to say that investigators have been lying about facts of the case and their cooperation levels from day one as well. They've stated time and again that they believe their son was kidnapped, despite it being nearly impossible for someone to get in or out of that particular part of the campground, where they were camping and where DeOrr went missing, without being seen by at least someone. Isaac Reinwand is an ex-convict so many people wonder if he played a role in the toddler's disappearance but it's important to note here that no one has ever been arrested in the case and there's no evidence to support what happened to DeOrr or who was ultimately involved one way or another. The police also named Robert Walton as a suspect and alleged that he has a history of domestic violence as well and feel he could have had a reason to hurt DeOrr because he was angry that Jessica and Vernal took the child away from him- whatever that means, no one really knows.

People in this community can't ignore the fact that this is a very small boy- a toddler- who seemingly vanished without a trace in the middle of the woods in the middle of nowhere with several adults around him. How did he so thoroughly vanish and in such a small window of time? After all, this isn't the first time we've seen something like this and with their being no other evidence ever found to this day, as more and more time passes, for some people it gets harder and harder to ignore the connections to other children who've gone missing in the same type of area and under the same bizarre circumstances. Was it something supernatural? Extraterrestrial? Nobody can say for sure and at the end of the day there's just as much chance of it being something like that as there is for something very mundane having been the culprit. Animal predation has been ruled out because there were no signs that anything like that happened. When an animal attacks anyone, a toddler especially, there's evidence left behind and even if no one saw anything, surely someone would have heard something. Did an accident happen that for one reason or another the family felt the need to cover it up? This case can become very convoluted when you let innuendo and rumor get in the way of the facts and the facts are no one has been arrested and there's not a single shred of evidence at all as to where this precious little boy went.

Vernal and Jessica broke up for good in 2016 and Jessica has since gotten married. They've both been vehement from the beginning that they have nothing to do with it and have no idea what happened to their little boy that day. In May of 2017 The National Center for Missing and Exploited Children released an age-progressed photo of what DeOrr Jr could possibly have looked like two years after he had gone missing at the age of 4 years old. They will continue to produce an age-progressed photo every 5 years. DeOrr's family affectionately called him "Little Man" and none of them will ever stop searching for him or for answers. They say he was curious, affectionate, and constantly happy. His grandmother, Tina Clegg, told East Idaho News recently, "We will do everything we can until the day we all die or find him."

The very small group of people who were with little DeOrr at the campsite the day he seemingly vanished into thin air are either telling the truth- in that they have no idea what happened to him or where he ended up, or they are hiding a deep, horrifying secret between themselves. Was he kidnapped, lost in nature, the victim of animal predation, the victim of other foul play or did he accidentally get hurt? Was it something else altogether? There's really no way of knowing but we hope that one day this mystery will be solved, one way or another, because this child- like so many others who end up vanishing without a trace- deserves for people to know what happened to him.

I always worry when discussing possible supernatural or paranormal elements involving the missing because let's face it, not everyone believes in this sort of thing and the last thing I would ever want to do is cause more pain for the loved ones of the missing who are left behind without any answers, but here's the thing- when everything else involving natural explanations have failed to turn up any evidence at all, I believe the only thing left to do is turn to the world of the supernatural in order to at least try and gain a better perspective at what we are dealing with in these particular cases. It's my personal opinion that it's more than likely the adults at the campground were telling the truth that day. In my book Missing: The Fae Theory, I talk about how the fae often will take or lure little children, especially ones that are too small to remember- like in DeOrr's case, out into the woods and take them to raise as their own. Either the fae sees something in the child's future that isn't too promising or very good, they see something in the child's parents and their energy they don't particularly like or they recognize their own blood in the child. Then, they take the child in the blink of an eye and before anyone around knows what happened and by the time the child is old enough to ask questions, he or she has no memory of the abduction or even of his or her own human parents. Sometimes the fae has lost their own child or their fae children would like a human playmate. I know that many people believe the fae only has bad or evil intentions when abducting humans and while normally that's the case with adults, it's not too often the likely reason for why they abduct a child. Most of the time the child in question will be described as either having perfect features, an exceptional intellect, or a very kind heart, when compared to other kids their age. This wouldn't just be a parent bragging about their own child and I've noticed in many of these cases it's even random people who've met the child on very few occasions that will say that there was just "something" about the child that struck them. I believe, in my own personal opinion, that DeOrr Kunz Jr. was taken by the fae and is living a beautiful, charming life in another dimension. Sometimes the fae will return a child to its human family once they're older and when they return they are often far more bright, beautiful, and gifted in some way artistically than other people their age. There might have been something else going on with that family or behind the scenes at that campground that made the fae feel like they needed to step in and take the child. At the end of the day though, just like with all of the strange cases in this book, that's just my educated guess and in the end we may never know the truth.

CHAPTER TWELVE

DAMING XU

On November 4, 2007, a mathematics professor at the University of Oregon named Daming Xu went out for a day hike in Willamette National Forest, right near Olallie Mountain, in Oregon. Despite being in his sixties at the time, Daming was known as a reasonably experienced hiker, and he was said to be in good physical condition. He had been out among and throughout those same trails dozens of times or more and he was very familiar with them. The trail he had chosen to hike that day was considered to be one that was particularly easy, with it being well traveled and the day being sunny, warm, and clear. For all of these reasons, it was even more odd when Daming didn't return from his trip when he was expected to. He had met with other hikers, Stephanie, and Paul Niedermeyer, along the hike route at around 1:30pm and both of them later reported that Daming appeared to be perfectly fine and in good spirits, though they admitted he seemed like he was in a big hurry for some reason. They would be the last people who ever saw him. When Stephanie and Paul returned to the trailhead parking lot they were surprised to see that Daming hadn't returned yet because he had set out ahead of them. They were worried to see that his vehicle was unattended and they were concerned enough to wait around until dusk to see if maybe he had been having trouble or if something else had gone wrong, but Daming never returned to his car. The young couple notified the authorities and a search was launched. It involved several agencies and infrared equipped aircraft, the entire area of the trail he had been on and everything that surrounded it was searched but no trace of the professor was ever found. Sniffer dogs did pick up his scent at one point and followed footprints thought to be his but the footprints and scent trail ended very abruptly and nothing was ever found. It was so bizarre that it's said to have confused the dogs and they no longer knew where to go. Inside of Daming's car the authorities found his cell phone and a survival kit. Either he thought he wouldn't need the survival kit due to the ease and his familiarity of the trail or he had simply forgotten it. They also, somewhat oddly, found only half of a trailhead guidebook. No one could figure out what possibly could have happened to him or where he had disappeared to but the weather was worsening by the day and eventually the search was called off due to the sudden dropping temperatures, as well as rain and snow. It didn't look good for Daming, who was seemingly still out there somewhere, among the trails and forest. The odds weren't in his favor that he would survive out there with the way the weather had so suddenly changed as he hadn't been prepared or equipped for anything more than a leisurely day hike under ideally calm conditions. He had no backpack, was carrying only one bottle of water and he only wore a light jacket.

It wasn't until eleven days after he had initially gone missing that any sign of him would be found. The other half of his trail guide was found lying on the ground in a treacherous and rocky, thickly wooded and very steep area that was very far off the designated trail he had initially been hiking along. There are so many questions left unanswered in this case, mainly- why would he have gone to that particular area so far off the trail in the middle of the day? How could he have gotten lost despite having the portion of the book with the trail map in it and speaking of the trail map- why had he only brought half of it with him? How was it that tracker dogs were unable to follow his scent and there were many other hikers in that particular area the day he disappeared so if he was in trouble or injured in some way, then why hadn't he just called out to one of them for help? Why hadn't he called out for help in general? If he had called out, he would have been heard. It's widely assumed that Daming had simply gotten lost and succumbed to the elements when the bad weather set in but then, how did he get lost in the first place when he was so familiar with the area he had been in? There were no remains or any signs of his body ever found, so where did that go? Whatever the answers to those questions are, we probably will never know, but Daming Xu has never been heard from again, his body has never been found and his ultimate fate remains a bizarre mystery.

While all of those questions are very reasonable, I see them being asked time and time again, in case after case. Here we have another very smart and professional man who walked into the woods to do something perfectly usual and ordinary who never came out. All of the strange clues are also a big part of what I see when researching these cases all the time. In *Missing The Fae Theory*, I talk about my belief as to why, at least some of the time, sniffer dogs refuse to do their job and track a person or why they seemingly become very confused and just sort of chase their own tails. The inclement weather causing searches to be hindered or called off is another one on my check list for strange things happening surrounding a not so straightforward disappearance. Daming's case did raise my eyebrows just a little bit more than most of the others in this book because he had multiple strange things going on surrounding his disappearance. It wasn't only one thing that stood out to me where I could point at it and definitively say, "Okay, this is what I believe happened to Daming Xu." There are too many different elements here and for that reason I don't really have an educated guess as to what happened to him and can only say that I'm confident it was something supernatural, and that we more than likely won't ever figure it out. He's joined a very long list of people who have very well meaning and highly trained men and women out searching for him but no one is looking in a supernatural direction. No matter how experienced or dedicated someone is to finding answers in cases like these, if they refuse to think outside of the box, in my opinion at least, they don't stand a chance of ever finding out the truth. However, sometimes I wonder if maybe they know that but are just looking for an explanation most people can live with. At the end of the day there's still no information as to what happened to Daming and I think any one of several supernatural entities that lurk in the wilderness out there or even some that are otherworldly who I believe pop in and out when they notice someone who they want to take, for whatever reason, shows up there.

CHAPTER THIRTEEN
DALE BANKER

59 year old Dale Banker from Denver, Colorado went missing somewhere around Sunday, October 21, 2007-

which is said to be the earliest day he could have been considered as such. Dale went missing from the Chimney Rock area of western Grand County and while investigators and his family were hopeful at first, there's still been nothing found in this case to indicate what might've happened to him or where he ended up. Dale was considered an outdoor and hunting enthusiast who had been meticulous about making sure he had all of the proper licenses and all of the best, most modern equipment whenever he set out into the woods. An alarm was raised when other hunters in the area found his guns, camping equipment and other personal belongings left inside of Dale's locked vehicle which was parked on Forest Service Road 103 in Chimney Rock. Located in western Grand County, that particular area is said to be extremely haunted by ghosts of the missing and all kinds of specters, good and bad and that's at least according to the locals. Whether or not that had anything to do with what happened to Dale remains a mystery as nothing more than what was in his vehicle was ever found of him.

    The hunters who found Dale's vehicle and belongings called the authorities and the report was then forwarded to the local office of the Colorado Division of Wildlife, as it was called back then. Today it's known as just Colorado Parks and Wildlife. CP&W investigated immediately into the alleged disappearance and found that there were witnesses who had come forward and reported seeing a man who matched Dale Banker's description sitting inside of the vehicle on the afternoon of October 21st. He was never seen again after that and because there was heavy snowfall that evening, investigators presumed the worst but tried to keep hope alive. They went so far as reporting two months later, in December of that same year, that they still thought Dale's case was that of a missing hunter who was alive but possibly injured in the forest somewhere. They believed because of his enthusiasm for the sport of hunting and his plethora of experience with being out in the wilderness for long periods of time, that he of all people would know how to survive for longer than the average person who didn't have that same background or know-how. Records show that the authorities conducted a thorough investigation of the vehicle itself but found no additional evidence or clues that would lead to Dale's whereabouts and there hadn't been any fresh tracks in the snow leading back to or anywhere near the vehicle, which would have shown that he had at least made it back there at some point.

Park officers knew their ability to investigate was more limited than the local sheriff's office would be and so, after they exhausted all of their own resources, they notified the local sheriff's office about Dale's case and aside from making additional sweeps of the area where the vehicle was found, they visited his home in Denver one time, but there was no one there to answer for them. They also reached out to several of Dale's closest friends and some of his acquaintances, but nobody had any additional information to give them about what could have possibly happened to Dale once he exited his vehicle on the twenty first. He had gone out there alone after all, and therefore there were no real witnesses to where he went when he left his vehicle or where he ended up. On October 28th, which was exactly one week from when the vehicle was found, the Grand County search and rescue got together with the sheriff's office and they joined forces and conducted a manhunt operation. Even with the help of numerous search dogs and while utilizing all of their many combined resources, they were never able to find a single clue or trace of what happened to Dale Banker. Eleven years after the official conclusion of the investigation into what had become of Dale Banker, in 2018, the police received a report that personal items, along with a human skull and some additional human bones, had been found at a ranch near Carter Mountain. The ranch was roughly about nineteen miles north of Kremlin, Colorado. The bones, particularly the skull, showed no signs of trauma and therefore the possibility of foul play was ruled out. Authorities suspected that the belongings and the remains belonged to Dale but it's unknown if they've identified them yet. As this had always been an open case, albeit a cold one, it was considered to be an ongoing investigation and the police involved in the investigation couldn't disclose many details of what was uncovered or even of what was specifically found.

Speculation persists that the bones did indeed belong to Dale Banker but there's no evidence that's been released to back that up. Even if the belongings and remains belonged to the missing hunter, it still says nothing about what could have possibly happened to him to lead him so far off of his intended course or how he had died, except to say that there most likely wasn't any foul play involved. However, I wonder if that can really be said. How would anyone really know whether or not foul play was involved in this case and who really defines what "foul play" actually means anyway. It's definitely not uncommon for hunters to go missing but I have a whole other theory about why that might happen. Think about it; if someone came onto your property- into your territory- with a gun, regardless of whether they were intending to do you harm or not and with you having no way of knowing their intentions- how would you react? Some states even have laws that allow a person to take lethal action against a trespasser in that situation. Aren't we all trespassers when we enter into the wilderness? How about when we accidentally enter into the territory of something otherworldly or supernatural- like in the case of inadvertently going through a portal or something similar? It's just something to think about- that's all I'm saying and in my opinion, it's just as reasonable as anything else that's been speculated about not only this case, but all of the others as well, up to this point.

CHAPTER FOURTEEN
ERIN MARIE GILBERT

Erin Marie Gilbert was described as a stunning, smart, and beautiful young woman by everyone who knew her. She was kind, loving, and a gregarious social butterfly. She knew what she wanted out of life from a very young age and though her main plans included attending cosmetology school, she was a writer at heart and an aspiring novelist. No one doubted a bit that she would eventually make that dream come true as well. In 1994 Erin made the move from San Francisco, California to Elmendorf Air Force Base (now known as Joint Base Elmendorf-Richardson), in Anchorage, Alaska in order to live with and help her sister Stephanie who had her own family there. Stephanie's husband was in the military and all of his extensive travel for work left his wife alone in Anchorage with their two children. Erin and Stephanie thought it would be a great idea and mutually beneficial for Erin to move in and help with the kids. The sisters were always close and that way they were able to be together and neither had to miss the other anymore. As far as everyone was concerned Erin was doing well and she was excited about her future. She found work right away as a nanny for a friend of Stephanie's.

Erin was only twenty-four years old and, naturally, she wanted to have a social life as well as being responsible with helping her sister and working as a nanny. It was while she was out one night at a bar she had been going to a lot since arriving in Anchorage called Chil-Koot Charlie's, Koot's for short, that she met a man named David Combs. It was the summer of 1995 and though they met and exchanged numbers in early June, they didn't really start talking or hanging out until they happened to run into one another again at the end of that same month, again at Koot's bar, and they really hit it off. They decided to have their first date on July 1st, the day after they had that random run in, at the Twentieth Annual Girdwood Forest Fair. That fair is an event held annually in Girdwood, Alaska and according to the website, "features Alaskan artists, hand-crafted items, exotic foods and entertainers from all over Alaska." David picked Erin up from Stephanie's house at four pm on the first of July. Erin's oldest nephew tried convincing her to take a cell phone with her but she didn't want to and eventually decided against it. Erin and David arrived at the fair about an hour later at five pm and shortly after that witnesses saw them together in the beer garden.

 According to David Combs, when he was later questioned by the authorities, the couple left the fair at around six that night, which was only one hour after they had gotten there in the first place. He said that he and Erin walked back to the car but when they got in, it wouldn't start. He claimed his battery had died because Alaska requires all drivers to "have headlights on where a roadway is posted to do so" and he gave the example of Seward Highway. He said that he had forgotten to turn them off when he and Erin left the car an hour earlier.

David told Erin that he had a friend who lived nearby and that he was going to walk to their house and get them to come and help him; possibly by giving his battery a jump. Erin wanted to stay in the car and wait for him to get back. David claims he walked around the area for almost two hours but was never able to find his friend's house. He finally decided to go back to his vehicle to check on Erin and give up his quest to find his friend's house after just a little over two hours but says Erin wasn't in the car or anywhere else for that matter when he returned. Ironically, he stated as well that the car started right up immediately when he tried it again once he got back. David just assumed that he had left her for too long by herself in the car and that she must've gone back out to the fair. He went so far as to say he searched the fair for another seven hours or so, until one in the morning the next day, but that he never saw her again.

The following day, July 2, 1995, he called Stephanie's house to make sure that she had gotten back safely. However, it was immediately obvious to Stephanie that her sister hadn't slept in her bed or been home at all since she had left the previous day with David. She immediately drove to Girdwood where she had the fair officials announce Erin's disappearance and name and then she and several other volunteers searched not only the fairgrounds but the nearby forest as well. When it was clear Erin was nowhere in the vicinity and that no one had seen or heard from her since the previous day, Stephanie called the local police in Girdwood and reported her as missing. She also notified local news media and got them to put Erin's photos and information, as well as details of her disappearance on the television news. Police conducted a thorough and extensive air and ground search but it was all to no avail and no sign or sight of Erin was ever found. Investigators originally considered the fact that Erin left voluntarily but her family was adamantly against that theory and vehemently denied any claims that she would have left her family of her own accord. They insisted they had a close knit family and that Erin never would have gone anywhere without letting at least someone know where she was going. Police then went on to consider that perhaps Erin had gotten tired of waiting for her date to come back and wandered off into the woods by herself to either try and find him or for some other unknown reason. Her family was also adamant that she never would have done anything like that, especially not with a fair full of people around, unless she was being chased by someone or something. There was no way possible, according to her family, that Erin had wandered ANYWHERE of her own accord, especially into the dense and isolated forest surrounding the fairgrounds.

Police started with David and questioned him several times. However, his story never changed and he remained immoveable about all of it, including where and how he had left Erin that day. It was thought to be odd by the family and investigators that David Combs never participated in any of the searches for Erin, aside from the initial one on the morning she went missing and he refused several offers to take a polygraph test in order to clear his name and back up his story. No other witnesses came forward to say that they had seen Erin either and the case almost instantly became a very frustrating one, not only for Erin's loved ones but for investigators as well. Stephanie made several trips back to Girdwood to search for her lost sister but never found any other clues or leads as to what could have possibly happened to her. She plastered Erin's missing person's flier all over- wherever she could- but all of her efforts were for nothing and the case eventually went cold.

In September of 2006 Stephanie and her family relocated to Washington but she never gave up her search for her sister and would occasionally, whenever she could, return to Alaska and search for her. In 2017 Erin's family offered a $37,000 reward for any information leading to the person responsible for her disappearance or her whereabouts. Although the police received a few tips, once followed up nothing ended up being relevant or substantial enough to get the investigation moving again. As of now Erin's case is assigned to the Alaska Bureau of Investigation's Cold Case Investigation Unit and while they aren't considering him a suspect, they would like to interview or speak with David Combs again. They claim that they have tried to contact him many times throughout the years since Erin's disappearance but he has not returned their phone calls and has otherwise made himself unavailable to them.

Erin Gilbert has been missing for almost three decades now and the police are no further in finding out what happened to her on that day so long ago, than they were the very first day they received the call that she had gone missing. When I first came across this case I couldn't help but notice the location. While Alaska is notorious for its untamed wilderness areas and places of the state that have never been set foot on by man, Erin was at a fairground with at least hundreds of people all over the place. Even in the parking lot, with people coming and going constantly, there should have been no time for someone to get to her and do anything harmful. She couldn't have been dragged away by a person or animals because someone would have seen or at the very least heard something, so what could have happened here? Alaska is more than well known in certain circles for being a somewhat odd place that is rife with supernatural and paranormal activity. There's something about the location, even within all of the beauty of Mother Nature, that seems to draw entities, creatures and beings from all different dimensions, realms, and worlds.

There isn't one thing I can point to here and say that I believe that thing is the most reasonable but I will say that there's a strong possibility that Erin was taken by something that moved quickly, silently, and invisibly through the woods and that somehow abducted or took her, without anyone noticing anything was amiss. Is there a possibility that a human being was involved? Sure, but that's the thing about it- there's almost always that possibility. The question I have to ask myself is how many times do we really expect a human being to be able to commit the absolute perfect crime and never get caught, even decades or sometimes centuries later? Humans are imperfect creatures but with everything supernatural and otherworldly already being reported as happening in Alaska at any given time of day, I think it would be remiss of us not to at least mention that extraterrestrials are everywhere in that state, mostly hidden under the vast waterways or deep underneath the earth. Whatever the case may be, unfortunately for

Erin and her family, I think unless they bring in some people who deal with supernatural abductions, and yes those people do exist, they won't ever come any closer to finding out what happened to their loved one. It's very unfortunate but I believe she was taken by either the fae or by extraterrestrials but as always there's no possible way for me to even take an educated guess as to which ones or why.

CHAPTER FIFTEEN

ALFRED BEILHARTZ

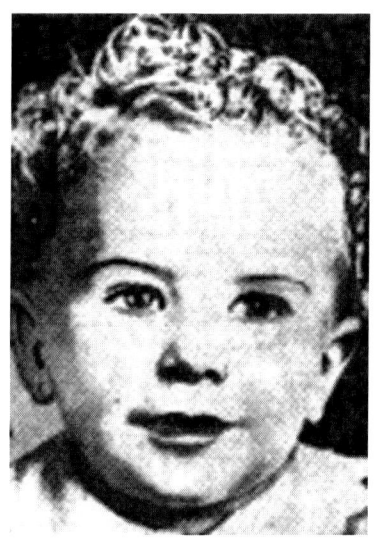

In the summer of 1938, four year old Alfred Beilhartz was at Rocky Mountain National Park in Colorado, on a fishing and camping trip with his family. It was Independence Day weekend and the Beilhartz family were simply enjoying each other's company and sometime in the great outdoors. They never imagined their family trip would be one of such great tragedy, and the mystery surrounding little Alfred's disappearance would be one that still endures almost a century later.

    The Beilhartz family, along with some family and friends who were with them for the trip, set up their camp about a quarter of a mile west of the Fall River Lodge. It was located just south of the west exit of the current Lawn Lake Trailhead parking lot. The camping party was located near where the Roaring and Fall Rivers met, just below Horseshoe Falls. The family woke up early in the morning and when his father William decided to walk down to a nearby stream to wash up, little Alfred decided to tag along. Family friends Oran Bronson and Walter Hansen also went to the stream to freshen up but they stopped at around five hundred feet upstream from Alfred and William in order to do so. William and Alfred finished up first and started to walk back to their camp. However, as William headed back to the camp, Alfred wanted to walk upstream to visit with Oran and Walter so that he could walk back to join the rest of his family with them once they were done.

    It wasn't long before the two men showed up back at

the camp but four year old Alfred wasn't with them or anywhere else to be seen. In the very short length of time, it was between when William had returned to camp and Oran and Walter came back as well, Arthur had seemingly vanished into thin air and without a trace. Immediately everyone began searching for Alfred and because of the short distance from the camp to the stream and the fact that there were over a dozen campers in their party alone, they figured they would find the little guy quickly. However, that isn't how it went at all. They all shouted his name and left no stone unturned and when that didn't turn up any sign of him, his parents decided to contact the park's service for help. Ranger Moomaw of the Fall River Ranger's Station responded right away and he immediately contacted the CCC, the Civilian Conservative Corps. The CCC is a work relief program that was created as part of then President Roosevelt's New Deal. Within just forty five minutes, more than one hundred CCC members had arrived to assist in the search for Alfred. On Monday the fourth of July, the CCC, the family and many other volunteers were still combing not only the area where Alfred went missing but also the surrounding areas. They continued to do so without any luck. Bloodhounds were brought in from the Colorado State Prison in order to also assist in the search but still no one was able to locate the boy or any clues to his whereabouts.

From the very beginning the rangers were working under the assumption that Alfred had drowned after falling into the nearby Roaring River. On July fifth, after still having no luck at all, they damned and diverted that river. Despite their efforts nothing was ever found and they eventually just erected a wire nearby to the Fall River in order to collect any evidence that might eventually show up. Eventually, after none of those efforts had turned up anything at all, they gave up searching the river altogether and moved on. Alfred's parents were insistent from the beginning that their son had been abducted. They knew with absolute certainty that the boy wouldn't have wandered too far from his family and were adamant that he hadn't gone near enough to the water to have been able to have fallen into the river. Searchers were frustrated and confused by their declarations but they continued to search the land anyway. By Thursday July seventh, more than two hundred searchers were scouring the land for him and they all told local news reporters that they wholeheartedly believed that the boy had either been abducted or had gotten lost in the forest. They were convinced as well that he hadn't drowned at all. The searchers explained their assumptions by telling the reporters that there was no way the little four year old boy could have passed all five of the beaver dams and reached the Fall River. They explained as well that, on the off chance that he had done just that, there was no way possible that he could have also passed the wire net set up near the Fall River by workers for the public service company of Colorado.

As far as the dogs brought in from the penitentiary, they did catch a human scent but immediately halted and stopped tracking once they reached the river. Under ordinary circumstances that would mean whoever the person was, had fallen into the river. Which, at that point, no one believed Alfred had done. On Sunday July third a radio appliance salesman named William J. Ells and his wife were also out for a hike in the Rocky Mountain National Park. They made it pretty far up Old Fall River Road when they stopped to take a break and catch their breath. It was around one in the afternoon and they decided to take a look up Mount Chapin when they got the shock of their lives. They told authorities later on that they saw a young boy sitting there on a rock in a section of mountainside known as Devil's Nest. They said the child made "a shrill noise" and was either pulled or fell back from the edge of the ledge. Devil's Nest is located approximately six miles from where Alfred Beilhartz was last seen by his family. The couple immediately started hiking up to where they saw the child because they felt the need to make sure that he was not only okay but not by himself and being properly supervised. However, once they finally reached the boulder he had been seen sitting on, he was gone and nowhere in sight. They decided then that it was imperative they let someone know a small, young child was seemingly wandering around Devil's Nest, possibly lost and unsupervised.

They hiked back to their vehicle and as soon as they got inside they heard a report on the news about the missing four year old near that area. When they arrived home they saw a photo of Alfred in the local paper and were positive that it was the same little boy they had seen sitting on that boulder. They promptly drove back to the park and alerted the rangers of what they had witnessed. The rangers were skeptical almost to the point of disbelieving the couple, as they thought it would have been impossible for such a young child to have wandered that far off in such a short period of time. They eventually decided to look more into it though and sent about one hundred and fifty searchers to the Devil's Nest area to check and see if any clues could be found but once again they came back empty handed. On July eighth the FBI announced that it was performing forensic testing on a piece of "soiled" bandage that had been found in an abandoned cabin inside of the park. This fact made Alfred's parents even more adamant that he had been abducted because his mother said she had bandaged a blister on his foot that had been bleeding with similar material as to what the FBI had found. On the same day the examination of the bandage was announced by the FBI, a woman named Mrs. Lynch, who lived in Big Spring, Nebraska, said she saw Alfred Beilhartz walking with a strange looking man along the highway as she and her husband made their way from Ogallala, Nebraska back to Big Springs. However, she didn't know what she had been looking at until she saw Alfred's picture and the news of his disappearance in the newspaper the next morning. She immediately alerted the authorities and said there was no doubt in her mind that the young boy she had seen was Alfred. Nothing ever came from this sighting, though it was investigated, and it hasn't ever been confirmed whether or not the little boy she saw was in fact Alfred Beilhartz.

On Sunday November 28th, five months after Alfred had gone missing and with no evidence ever found to lead to where he ended up or had gone to, William Beilhartz woke up to find a ransom demand for his son. The message said, "Sorry for your son. We went west. Out of money. The boy doesn't take to us. We will return your son if you leave $500 in a can one block from your house and the note. We will return your son within 24 hours." However, it only took one day for investigators to discover that the note was merely a cruel joke or left by someone who needed money and decided to try and extort a grieving and desperate family in order to get it. Nothing ever came of the note and it was almost immediately deemed a fake and unrelated to the case.

So, what happened to Alfred Beilhartz? Did he drown in the river as the police initially suspected? Was he abducted as his parents have always maintained? Was there some sort of cover up by the family who were out there with him that day? Did some accident befall Alfred and then his family or their friends decide it would be easier to cover it all up instead of coming clean? The main line of thought for this case is that if he had gotten lost or something else had happened to him inside of the park, including if he had drowned, surely in the last seventy eight years since it happened there would have been SOME evidence that turned up. However, there has never been a single shred of evidence as to where Alfred ended up or what happened to him, leading most people nowadays who look at the case to believe he was abducted. I tend to be of the same mindset but I don't think it was a human being who took Alfred.

Throughout the stories in this book, these real cases, we keep seeing the same scenario and set of circumstances time and time again and never in any of those cases, and thousands more that we haven't discussed yet, is anyone ever found or does any evidence lead to anything substantial that could show what happened to them. It's heartbreaking but I believe there are forces both above and below the earth that are much more powerful and much wiser than we are as mere human beings and that some of them, for whatever reason, take/abduct human beings from time to time. There are entities that live underground, that are cloaked in ships in the sky above us, both inside and outside of our atmosphere, and there are also entities all around us simply blending in with our society. Out in the woods, and it seems for whatever reason in National Parks and areas like them in particular, that there is a lot of strangeness in the energy. Whatever is orchestrating these disappearances has the ability to cause inclement and show stopping weather, to make dogs whose literal job it is to search out clues not want to do that and seemingly also to make those same animals become confused as though they don't know what they're searching for anymore. I keep reiterating that I can't put my finger on and definitively state in any of these cases exactly what it is that's taking each individual person but I can definitely say that I believe the possibilities are endless and far beyond the scope of what our imaginations are capable of conjuring up.

CHAPTER SIXTEEN

MICHAEL DAVID VAN ZANDT

Michael David Van Zandt was a thirty six year old father of three when he went missing. On March 15, 2016, the Air Force veteran decided to go out with some friends to party and blow off some steam. That night he and his friends watched the UFC fight at The Underground Bar at Pier Plaza and because the drive from where they were in Hermosa Beach was such a long drive from Lancaster, where they all lived, they decided to check into the Quality Inn Hotel which is located on the 900 block of Aviation Boulevard. Michael got separated from his friends and was last seen by his friends leaving a long line at the American Junkie Restaurant because he needed to use the bathroom at around 10:15 pm. He walked to the liquor store next door to the restaurant and several cameras captured him going in and out. His friends left to go somewhere else and tried to call his cell phone a total of twenty two times but each time they received no answer and they were never able to get a hold of him. Another surveillance camera captured Michael going back to the line at the restaurant and looking for his friends but when he wasn't able to locate them he turned and walked back into the liquor store but it's unclear if he purchased anything at that time. Then he walked outside, walked away, and was never seen or heard from again. The last footage of him shows him, at approximately 11:27pm walking northwest through a parking lot, heading towards a bench. Then, he just seemingly vanished into thin air.

His friends went back to the hotel room at around one in the morning and waited for him until 1 o'clock the following day, which brings us to Sunday afternoon and approximately fifteen hours since anyone had seen or heard from Michael. When his friends checked the parking lot of the hotel they saw that his vehicle was still parked in the same spot and none of his belongings had been disturbed. This was when his friends started calling jails and hospitals in the local area, fully expecting him to have ended up somewhere, drunk, and maybe in a little bit of trouble. However, their search yielded no luck and they were unable to find out where he had gone. Michael worked for the Edwards Air Force Base but he did not show up for work on Monday morning as he was scheduled to do. One of the friends that had been out with him the previous Saturday night also worked with him and when Michael didn't show up for his shift, he called the authorities and reported him as missing. A search was immediately launched but the dogs brought to track his scent lost him right near the liquor store where he was last seen. They didn't find any of his belongings on the beach and no witnesses, people who were on the beach or in the general vicinity of it that night, remembered him having gone into the water.

    His credit and debit cards have been inactive since that first night he was gone and his cellphone activity stopped at around 10:30 pm on that same night. Michael and his wife, Krishain Van Zandt were going through a divorce at the time of his disappearance but even she admitted there's no way he would have ever just up and left his children this way. Nobody who knew him believes he left voluntarily and just walked away from his life. Michael's brother Tyler had repeatedly expressed concern that he fears his brother may have tried to go for a swim. He told ABC7 News, "He's somebody that does like to take swims at night, you know, after he's been drinking?" Michael Van Zandt is described as a Caucasian male and stands at six feet tall, weighing one hundred and ninety pounds. He has multiple tattoos which include a small Buddha on his back, the word KEATON in descending letters on his left calf and a tiger and jungle scene on his upper left arm. He is classified as endangered missing and he would be forty three years old today. He was last wearing a long sleeved dark gray sweatshirt or sweater over a white shirt, blue jeans and shoes or boots. He has blonde hair and blue eyes and his nickname is Mike.

Here we have yet another case of a perfectly healthy young man going missing after a night out drinking with his friends. What made this case stand out to me is that Michael had actually gone missing DURING a night out with his friends. There's a lot of speculation that perhaps he was too intoxicated to realize that it wasn't a good idea to go for a swim that night and he drowned.

But what if something else happened to him? Let's say he did end up in the water, which I absolutely think is possible here, then what was it that drew him there? Sure, he was known to love night swimming and as a person who never really quite feels like I fit in anywhere until I'm on a beach and feel the ocean waves at my feet, I can totally understand that but what if he was drawn there and then taken by whatever it is that's living in the depths of our oceans? There's been evidence in the form of eyewitnesses and encounters from people who have been in crafts that they either saw coming out of a large water source, like the ocean, or that they were abducted and brought into the sea themselves. I believe many of these witnesses and have even talked to people that have felt compelled to walk into the sea at night, specifically while on vacation and also, I've talked to people who have walked in, tentatively, to investigate strange lights that seemed to be shining from within the ocean itself. It's not an uncommon thing if your eyes are very open and you know where to look. Just like with every other case I've covered in this book; I hope and pray that this man's family gets answers and finds a truth they can live with. However, in most of these cases, I believe something supernatural or otherworldly is at play and unfortunately most of the public doesn't have access to exactly what any of it is or means at this point in time.

CHAPTER SEVENTEEN
PHILIP KREYCIK

Let's talk about another aspect of all of these missing persons cases where they seemingly vanish without a trace in the literal blink of an eye and that's when they are clearly heard calling for help from somewhere in the area where they were thought to have gone missing from, only to end up never being found, even despite various agencies and numerous volunteers looking for them. This isn't just one or two or even a handful of cases either. This happens all the time. People go out for what seems like a pleasant and scenic hike and end up not ever being seen or heard from again- aside from the desperate calls for help heard far and wide. Take thirty seven year old Philip Kreycik from Berkely, California. Philip told his wife he was headed out for a run in the hills near Moller Ranch staging area in Pleasanton Ridge Regional Park in California. This wasn't anything unusual and there was no reason for his wife to think it would be the last time she ever saw him.

    He called her once he reached the trail to inform her it would take him about an hour and to let her know when she could expect him back that day. He was last seen running at around 10:45 am that same morning. Philip's wife reported him as missing the same afternoon he had headed out for the run, when he failed to return home and hadn't been in contact with her or anyone else to let them know why he wasn't back yet, which was very unlike him by all accounts. Investigators in Pleasanton stated that they had never come across such a bizarre case. Either he got hurt and was only able to call out or he planned all of this and purposely disappeared, leaving his life behind and never looking back. Leaving his family and friends to wonder forever what happened to him and why. According to his family, the latter isn't even an option as Philip just wasn't that type of man and loved his life. Philip was supposed to meet with his wife to attend a family gathering in Stockton two hours after he had initially started out on his run. His wife immediately knew something was wrong and called the authorities when he didn't show up or contact anyone.

Philip is said to have left his shirt and cellphone in his vehicle and although he was running with a smart watch, it was unfortunately not equipped with GPS. Temperatures rising above one hundred degrees that day in Pleasanton led many to immediately begin to speculate that the heat had somehow incapacitated him. That was on July 10, 2021. This theory didn't make much sense to his family and loved ones though as Philip was a marathon runner and was well adjusted to running under such extreme conditions as blaring heat which may incapacitate most people. His cellphone showed that his route was planned out, entirely along very well maintained and manicured trails. Though the park was packed with people that day, not a single credible sighting of Philip has ever been reported. "I can't even speculate on this one. It's very very odd." said Sgt. Aaron Fountain of the Pleasanton police department, who is handling the investigation. Philip Kreycik was a family man with two small children, not to mention a graduate of the prestigious Harvard University in Boston, Massachusetts. He was also listed as a third year student in MIT's Urban Mobility Lab.

Philip went missing on a Saturday, the following Wednesday a family hiking in the area reported hearing cries in a canyon near Sunol Post Office. After receiving this tip, two people who were involved in the search went out to the area and heard for themselves a man screaming for help near the canyon. Experienced hikers in the search and rescue effort set out to go and see if they could hear the calls and perhaps follow them to try and find Philip and bring him safely back to his family. However, once arriving at the spot where the cries for help were allegedly heard by multiple people at this point, they heard nothing and weren't able to locate Philip either. That same night the search efforts were officially called off and Philip hasn't yet been found and who knows if he ever will be. Theories run wild as to what happened to Philip Kreycik. From demented and murderous drug dealers taking him hostage to large felines somehow carrying him up trees and feasting, to him just walking off and abandoning his life, which he was said to love so much. However, that's just what these are, theories and there isn't even any evidence as to if this was definitely Philip who was head crying from the canyon for help that fateful day either. Why didn't the first two experienced hikers who were sent out and did claim to have heard at least someone crying for help never find him? This is another case that is completely and totally baffling and runs along the exact same vein as the previous two and the cases to follow, we will never know. Surely if he was attacked and eaten by wildlife there would have been some sort of trail for either the animal searchers or even the human ones to find and follow, at least leading to some sort of explanation.

The fact of the matter is it's been reported more often than the average person would like to believe that people call out after accidentally walking into some sort of portal or time rift. I know it will sound crazy to most people who read this book but I'm telling you it's true. Sometimes people see the portal in front of them and get too curious, never to be seen or heard from again. However, I've come across several instances of people who survived actually going through a portal and it's almost always a very terrifying experience that changes the life of the person who experienced it forever. The reason this case has me stuck on the idea that it's more than likely a portal is because he was clearly heard calling out for help. While it's true that no one can be sure that it was him calling out that day, who else would it have been? To the best of my knowledge no one ever came forward and told the authorities that it had actually been them calling out on that day at that exact time and why. People who have walked through portals, particularly in the woods, have often come forward later on and said that while they could see and hear the search and rescue workers all around them, it seemed like the workers couldn't see and could barely hear them. It's almost like once you walk through one of these portals of time rifts, which are two very different things by the way and they each have a very different effect and consequence, you cease to exist in this reality as we know it and exist instead in the world all around us that most of the human population not only can't see, but that they aren't aware of to begin with.

CHAPTER EIGHTEEN

KENNETH SCOTT REED

Born on July 31, 1964, Kenneth Scott Reed dropped out of high school in the eighth grade he joined adult schools to try to obtain an equivalency diploma but because of his dedication to the job he was working at the time, for

Bee Bee Dairy, he wasn't able to keep up with the work. He started working at a restaurant called The Dairy in 1981 and had started working there as a dishwasher. Since he was such a dedicated and hard worker, he quickly rose the ranks at the Dairy and became an assistant manager. Everyone who knew him, including his many coworkers, said that Kenneth was fun loving and responsible and before he went missing he had a perfect attendance record at his job and hadn't ever missed a single day in eight years. Until that is, he went missing. Kenneth shared a roommate at his apartment on Halls avenue in Colchester but often stayed the night at his parent's house because it was so much closer to his beloved job. His mother was disabled and even when he wasn't spending the night in order to go to work the next morning, being the wonderful and caring son that he was, Kenneth also stopped by to see his parents for no reason too. Ray Skidgel was a longtime friend of Kenneth Reeds and he would tell investigators that sometimes Kenneth got bored with his job at the dairy and would occasionally become depressed, but that it never lasted very long. Ray said that Kenneth would also say to him, "Ray, I don't know", which presumably meant that he didn't know what to do with his life and/or that he wasn't sure about continuing to work at his job. It's unknown exactly what Kenneth meant when he said those sorts of things to his friends because there was no elaboration given with the quotes. Kenneth had no criminal record or history, loved sports and was known as something of a ladies man, though he hadn't had a steady girlfriend in several years at the time of his disappearance. In the week before Kenneth disappeared he was threatened twice. The first time was on March sixteenth when he approached someone who had worked at the Dairy restaurant for many years but whom Kenneth had chosen to fire. The man agreed to resign by the end of the week but he wasn't happy about it and ended up making threats towards Kenneth because of the altercation. However, the employee started to become very aggressive, throwing things around the restaurant and at Kenneth himself and so he was asked to leave by Ken, who was the manager at the time. Kenneth had also been threatened around that same time by the new boyfriend of a woman he had previously dated. It's unclear, but some people speculated that Kenneth had dated the woman while she was still dating the other man, the one who had made the threats, but that's never been proven. The woman said she had spoken to Kenneth a short while before he had disappeared and that he told her he was depressed but that he didn't elaborate as to why.

On March 24th, 1989, Kenneth clocked out of work

as usual at 3:26pm. The manager at the restaurant, a man named Michael Thorne, said that although Ken seemed tired, he expressed his excitement for an upcoming ten day vacation he had planned for himself. His brother Donald said that Ken had consulted with Sunnyside of Travel, which was an agency in Ledyard, CT, but that he hadn't made any formal arrangements to go anywhere. Kenneth also hadn't mentioned that he was planning on going anywhere during his ten day vacation to anyone in his family and they all believe that's something he definitely would have told them. The manager noted that though he didn't think it was too strange at the time, after all was said and done and Kenneth was officially a missing person, he realized it was odd that five acquaintances of Ken Reed's had come into the restaurant to speak to him the last day he was there. None of those people had ever come in there before and so thinking back he thought it was very strange. Kenneth told Michael that he would be in to work forty five minutes early the next day to help him with the general daily duties at the restaurant. One of the waitresses there, a woman named Jeanne Bessett, said that on his last day of work Kenneth had agreed to meet her and several other work acquaintances at the Norwich Sheraton that night but that he never showed up. It had been pouring rain all day long so they all thought he simply didn't want to go out in that weather. After he clocked out and left his job for the day, Kenneth stopped and got himself a coffee at a nearby donut shop and then went to his parent's house in Norwich, CT. Kenneth's father saw him parking his gray, four door Isuzu I-Mark in front of their house but he went back inside quickly before Kenneth came in, due to the heavy rainfall. Kenneth never made it inside his parent's house though and he hasn't been seen or heard from since.

Kenneth Scott Reed had seemingly disappeared off the face of the earth within fifteen minutes of leaving his job. Either a neighbor or a friend who was living with the family, there are sources that say both, noticed that Kenneth's car was left parked but blocking his parent's cars in the driveway. Ray Skidgel said, "When it comes to his coffee, no matter what the circumstances, he will drink his coffee" and was seemingly referencing the fact that the coffee was left un-drunk in or on top of the vehicle. Ray also made comments telling investigators that Ray never blocked his parent's driveway and that he always locked his car doors, which made it all even stranger as he had blocked the driveway that time and left the vehicle unlocked just before he disappeared. There was no indication that any struggle had taken place at the scene. Kenneth wasn't reported as missing until three days after he actually disappeared, and that report was made on the twenty seventh of March. His parents explained that they had waited because they thought that he might have just been with friends or had gone off for a few days with a woman. They said that although Kenneth often left without telling anyone, he would always show back up within a day or two but that this time everything was different and so many things just seemed "off." Those closest to him reported that Ken seemingly had no personal problems and that he didn't seem to be afraid of anyone in the days leading up to his disappearance. He didn't have any issues with substance abuse and it was very much out of character for him to just leave and take off for days without telling anyone about it. Kenneth's brother Donald took three weeks off of work once his brother was officially reported as missing and he spent that whole time looking for him. He called and communicated with the media to get the word out and he also consulted a psychic who claimed to have had two visions of the missing man. One Psychic's vision was about him being in a blue Plymouth Valiant and another said he was in a blue Firebird. Law enforcement interviewed and spoke with about a total of twenty people, most of them Kenneth's friends and family members. They searched all over Norwich and investigated the threats Ken had received in the week leading up to his disappearance. Two and a half weeks after he went missing the police took two German shepherds with them to the woods to search along a river near his parent's home. There had been previous searches done by friends and family in that area but nothing had come from them and the searches of that area by police with the dogs also hadn't yielded any evidence. They eventually searched the banks of the Yantic River but no evidence was found there either. Law enforcement released a nationwide bulletin regarding Kenneth's disappearance and they even searched several areas using helicopters but no clues as to where Kenneth had disappeared had been uncovered.

On November 24th, Kenneth was profiled on Crime Stoppers 800. The show was broadcast to 125 television stations, or eighty seven percent of the US. The show followed Connecticut State Police Detective Larry Gilbeault as he retraced the last known details of the events that led to Kenneth's disappearance. It also included a reenactment of the crime. He commented: "This man has been missing for nineteen months with no trace whatsoever. In the fifty or sixty people we've talked with, we haven't come up with anything. We're just trying to perk up interest in the case and keep people talking about it." His mother, Esther, said she had no interest in watching it and said, "I'm not going to watch it because I'll break." She said it was just too painful for her to have to think about and relive the whole experience. It had been approximately eight months since Kenneth had first gone missing and she couldn't deal with another let down. She said she had too many remaining questions, and his smile haunted her. Matt James, the executive producer, said the show had a forty percent chance of producing more information. Nothing ever came of those efforts and Kenneth's disappearance still eluded everyone involved. Law enforcement officials still believe there's a chance that foul play is involved in his disappearance but there's been no evidence to prove or disprove that there was. There's simply nothing to go on and every lead turns up nothing new. Cindy Paquette works for Bee Bee Dairy in Waterford, CT and is the woman who originally hired Kenneth as a dishwasher when he was just sixteen years old and she commented about the case that, "Nothing ever made sense. I saw him grow from a young kid into a very responsible adult. He wasn't into drugs. He wasn't a playboy by any means. He was an inner city kid who made it out. At the time, he was due for a vacation." Lawrence read was quoted as stating, "I think he's alive out there someplace. He doesn't strike me as someone who can be taken out that easily." Kenneth left behind a brand new stereo system and his bank account has never been touched after he went missing. His vacation pay is still waiting for him to this day. Kenneth Scott Reed is a Caucasian male and described as having "A dark complexion." At the time of his disappearance, he weighed between one hundred and forty and one hundred and fifty pounds, was described as having a medium build and stood at 5'8" tall. He had blonde hair and brown eyes. When he went missing he had a dark colored mustache. Though dental and fingerprint records aren't available in this case, DNA records are. He is fifty nine years old as of February 2024 and was last seen wearing gray pants and white Nike Air Jordan sneakers with blue stripes. He is classified as an endangered missing person.

I specifically wanted to include this case in this book to show that these types of disappearances don't only happen when someone is out and about in the wilderness. It happens in all different types of places, all over the world, every single day. Could this case have some foul play involved, absolutely, but there's also something else to consider. How did this whole grown man just seemingly evaporate into thin air while exiting his vehicle? He left behind his favorite beverage and left his car sort of just sitting there. To me this seems like a case where he got out of his car, possibly because he saw something strange, and had every intention of getting back into the vehicle and parking it properly as he always did and of drinking his coffee. This could very well be another case of an abduction by one of the cloaked extraterrestrial ships that hover just inside and oftentimes just above our atmosphere. I wish I knew what it was about the missing that are abducted by extraterrestrials that they are the ones chosen. Or could it be that they're just victims of opportunity and circumstance? Maybe he saw the craft or a being- he could have seen anything- and he slowly tried to make his way to see what it was that he was looking at and then he was taken. I can't say for sure, obviously, but this one really made me think about how little most of the world's population really knows about what's out there, all around them, that they aren't even aware of, and that is such a danger to them and the lives they're living.

Thank you for reading. If you enjoyed consider reading my other books. They can be found on Amazon.

ABOUT THE AUTHOR

Gemma Jade was born and raised in Passaic County, New Jersey and has always felt drawn to the paranormal and supernatural world. She saw her first full bodied apparition at the age of four and was more interested in than terrified of it. Once she was old enough she started to seek answers. Gemma is of Native American and Irish descent and was fascinated by the old legends from both countries. She first encountered the fairies and their magic when she was 7 and her paternal grandmother from the Irish old country would tell her of the myths and legends of "the Little Ones." Gemma was and continues to be lured by the unknown. She is also a clairvoyant and clairsentient psychic and credits this to her native American blood. She currently resides in Morris County, New Jersey.

Gemma has taken her research and search for all things paranormal, supernatural and unexplained to her youtube channel titled simply Gemma Jade. She has joined with Steve Stockton to livestream and communicate with other like minded individuals who are searching for the truth. They talk a lot about the missing in the woods, and of course the fae. Gemma's focus on her channel is also to bring light to missing person's cases happening all over the world both inside and out of the woods. She has even given a platform to her viewers where they cannot only feel safe in telling their own encounters, but also where they can communicate with like minded individuals in her community.

Join Gemma on her channel here: https://www.youtube.com/c/GemmaJadeYT

ALSO BY GEMMA JADE

Missing: The Fae Theory

Shadow Entities: Sleep Paralysis and Beyond

Encounters with Evil: 101 True and Terrifying Stories

Danger at Your Door: Encounters with Black Eyed Kids

Midnight Visitors: True Stories of Black-Eyed Kids

Campfire Stories: Encounters in the Woods (Series)

Made in United States
North Haven, CT
12 December 2024

62256756R00112